P pillsbury publications

Pillsbury's Bake-Off Cookie Book

Shortcutted prize winning favorites from 18 years of Bake Offs

Dear Homemaker:

*A cookie jar filled with freshly baked cookies
will win praise from your family and their friends.
Their happy smiles are your reward.*

*Keeping the cookie jar filled to satisfy the appetites
of growing youngsters can take a good deal of
your precious time. That is why we have taken the
favorite cookie recipes of American homemakers
from the last 18 years of the Bake-Off and short-cutted
them with time-saving ingredients and methods
so that keeping the cookie jar filled will be a
breeze for you and a joy for your children.*

*Our collection of treasured cookies includes not
only cookie jar favorites you can whip up in
minutes but hardy travellers for the lunch box
or picnic basket, traditional holiday cookies for
gatherings or giving, fancy cookies for party
times as well as cookie desserts for
company and family.*

*Crisp, cakey, candy-like or nutty, we've tried
to please all the cookie lovers in your
family and we hope you'll enjoy the
pleasures of baking these recipes.*

Cordially yours,

Ann Pillsbury

Contents

Facts

• We might never have enjoyed the delights of cookies as we know them if the fire-heated ovens of our ancestors had the accuracy of our modern ovens of today. History first recorded cookies as being test cakes made from small amounts of cake batter to judge the heat of the oven. Indeed the very name cookie is derived from the Dutch word "koekje" meaning "little cake."

The endless number of cookie recipes gives testimony to the enduring popularity of these little cakes yet in spite of the array of flavors and textures, there are only six basic kinds of cookies. These are: drop, bar, rolled, molded, pressed and refrigerator.

Drop cookies are the quickest and easiest to make. The dough is usually mixed in one bowl and dropped by spoonfuls onto a cookie sheet. Use two teaspoons (not measuring spoons), spooning up the dough with one and pushing it onto the baking sheet with the tip of the second. The size of the cookie depends upon the size of the spoonful of dough and should be kept uniform. The dough should be fairly soft. Since these cookies usually spread during baking, keep them about 2 inches apart unless the recipe directs otherwise. Recipes for drop cookies usually provide a large quantity and are ideal for filling the cookie jar.

Bar cookies and squares are also among those quick and easy to prepare. They are usually made from a soft dough and baked in a shallow square or rectangular pan. These may be a cake-type cookie such as brownies or may be layered with different textures and flavors. Chopped nuts, coconut or oatmeal may be used to give texture to the bottom layer or topping which frequently has a fruit filling in the center. Bar cookies can also double as dessert squares when cut into larger portions and topped with whipped cream or ice cream.

Rolled cookies are made from a stiff dough which is rolled out and cut with sharp cookie cutters, a knife or pastry wheel. The cookies should be thin and crisp. Chill the dough if it is too soft to handle easily. It is usually best

Chocodiles — Bar Cookie

Date Jewel Drop — Drop Cookie

Caramel Crisps — Rolled Cookie

to work with a small amount of dough at a time rolling it out on a lightly floured bread board or pastry cloth. A floured stockinet cover on the rolling pin will also help keep the dough from sticking. Use as little flour as possible. Dip cookie cutters in flour each time before cutting dough to prevent sticking. Save all the trimmings and reroll these at one time as these cookies will be less tender.

Molded cookies are made with a stiff dough and shaped into balls, "logs", crescents or sticks. The dough is more easily handled if it is well chilled and your hands are well floured. For many cookies the "balls" are flattened with the palm of your hand or the bottom of a glass which has been greased and dipped in flour, granulated or confectioners' sugar.

Butternut Balls — Molded Cookie

Spicy Spritz — Pressed Cookie

Redip the glass for each cookie. A cut-glass with an interesting design on the bottom can give a very pretty pattern to the cookie. Some cookies such as peanut butter are usually given a criss cross design on top by flattening with the floured tines of a fork. If balls are to be dipped in confectioners' sugar after baking it is best to do so once while they are still warm and again after they have cooled.

Pressed cookies are formed by forcing the dough through a cookie press or pastry tube into different shapes. The dough is usually very rich and just soft enough to force through the tube. Since the dough is so rich it is often advisable to chill or even partially freeze the cookies before baking to minimize the amount they spread and help retain their shape during baking. Pressed cookies are usually party fare and may be decorated with candied fruit, sugar or nuts before or after baking.

Refrigerator cookies are the answer to having fresh cookies on a moments notice. They are usually made with a rich dough which is very stiff and shaped into long rolls one to two inches in diameter. Store in the refrigerator or freezer until ready to slice thin and bake. Fresh cookie dough in a variety of flavors is available in the grocer's dairy case that may be sliced and baked in the same way.

Pinwheel Butterflies — Refrigerator Cookie

Tips

Ingredients for cookies are basically flour, sugar, shortening, leavening, eggs and/or milk. They vary in proportion depending on the type of cookie made. All ingredients should be at room temperature in order to blend the dough more easily.

Pillsbury's Best All Purpose Flour has been used in developing all of these recipes and unless specified does not require further sifting. Be sure to follow measurements exactly because too much flour will result in dry, tough cookies. Spoon the flour loosely into the measuring cup and level with a spatula or back of a table knife.

Butter, margarine and shortening are often used interchangeably although at least some butter is recommended for the flavor it adds. Especially rich cookies such as pressed and molded cookies usually call for butter or a combination of butter and margarine.

Eggs used in testing these recipes were U. S. graded large which measure 5 to the cup. Always remember to separate the egg yolks and whites while they are cold. Let the egg whites come to room temperature before beating in order to make a meringue with the best volume and stability.

Chopped nuts, raisins, coconuts, spices and candied fruit may all be added to cookie dough to give variety in color, flavor and texture.

Equipment for cookie making should include standard nested measuring cups for measuring dry ingredients as well as a glass or plastic measuring cup for liquids. A standard set of measuring spoons is essential. Accurate measurement of ingredients is the first step to success in cookie baking.

A rolling pin and bread board with a pastry cloth and stockinet cover will help in making rolled cookies. A collection of interesting cookie cutters with sharp edges will give variety to the shapes you make.

An electric mixer is a time saver in mixing soft doughs and may be used through the first addition of flour for stiffer doughs.

Baking sheets should have little or no sides so the cookies bake quickly and evenly. Shiny

light metal pans or teflon coated pans give the best results. Dark metal pans will cause cookies to have an undesirable dark crust. Allow 2 inches clearance between the pan edges and the oven sides for circulation of heat and even baking. If you are baking two pans of cookies in the oven at the same time it is best to switch the pans once during baking for better browning. Do not grease cookie sheets unless the recipe calls for it, otherwise the cookies may spread too much during baking. Be sure the cookie sheet is cool before placing unbaked dough on it. Heat will cause the shortening to melt and the cookies to spread before they start baking.

Preheat the oven to the correct temperature before baking cookies and watch them carefully during baking because minutes can make quite a difference in the end product. Most recipes include a time range because of variations in ovens and the size and shape of the cookies. If you are baking an especially rich cookie it is wise to test bake a few to determine how much they will spread. If they seem to spread too much it may help to partially freeze the unbaked cookies before baking

them. Remember cookies continue to bake a few minutes after they come from the oven so it is best to remove them when they are lightly browned and just set in the center.

Cool cookies on a wire rack immediately after baking. Drop, rolled, molded and pressed cookies are best removed from the cookie sheet with a wide spatula. If they stick, return them to the oven for a few seconds until they can be easily removed. Bar cookies and squares are usually cooled in the pan and cut after they have cooled.

Storage. Store cookies after they have completely cooled. Soft cookies should be stored in a closely covered container so they do not dry out. A piece of bread or slice of apple will help retain moisture but should be replaced every few days. Crisp cookies are best stored in a container with a loosely fitting lid. If they soften in storage they may be made crisp again by placing in a 300° F. oven for about 5 minutes.

Glossary

This is not intended to be a complete glossary of baking terminology but rather an explanation of some of the less familiar terms to be found in these recipes to help you with your cookie baking.

a

almond paste — a paste made of finely ground blanched almonds and cane sugar.

b

bake — to cook by dry heat, usually in the oven.

baking powder — a mixture of acid, baking soda, and starch or flour which reacts in the presence of liquid and heat to produce gas that leavens batters and doughs.

baking soda — an alkali which reacts with an acid such as sour milk or molasses to form a gas that leavens batters and doughs.

batter — a mixture of flour, liquid and other ingredients which is thin enough to be poured or dropped.

beat — to mix with an over-and-over motion, using a spoon, rotary beater or electric beater. Of eggs—slightly beaten: just enough to mix yolk and white; well beaten: beat until light and foamy.
Of yolks—slightly beaten: just enough so that yolk loses its shape; well beaten: beat until thick and lemon colored.
Of whites—slightly beaten: beat until foamy; stiffly beaten: beat until thick and forms stiff peaks.

blanch — to immerse briefly in boiling water, usually followed by quick cooling in cold water. Also, to scald by pouring boiling water over a food, as almonds, to loosen the skin.

blend — to combine two or more ingredients thoroughly.

brown sugar — a sugar obtained by boiling cane syrup from raw sugar. The amount of molasses retained gives the sugar its color and flavor. Brown sugar is labeled golden brown, light brown, dark brown. The darker the color, the more molasses present in the product. Used in baking and candy making. Light or dark brown sugar is used to give a butterscotch flavor to cookies. Brown sugar must be firmly packed if ¼ cup or more is used. If granulated brown sugar is used refer to box label for substitute table.

c

caramelize — usually of sugar, to heat until it is melted and brown. Also, to heat food containing sugar until brown. Browning of the sugar achieves a distinctive flavor.

chocolate:

semi-sweet — semi-sweet cooking chocolate packaged in 1-ounce squares.

unsweetened — sometimes referred to as baking chocolate. Packaged in 1-ounce squares or 1-ounce envelopes of premelted chocolate.

German sweet chocolate — a sweet cooking chocolate available in ¼-pound bars.

coats spoon — leaves a thin, even film on a metal spoon which is dipped into the cooking mixture, removed and allowed to drain.

coconut — flaked, chopped, shredded, grated or finely grated are generic terms of commercially available forms of coconut which may be used when small pieces are required. Shredded coconut is sometimes referred to as "Southern Style" and is more often used as a topping or coating because of its long pieces. Toasted coconut is made by spreading any of the available types of coconut in a shallow pan and placing in a 350°F. oven until lightly browned. The coconut should be stirred frequently and watched closely for even toasting.

cream — to combine shortening, butter or other fat with sugar until the mixture is light and completely blended, or to soften one or more foods.

cut in — to use two knives, pastry blender or fork to distribute shortening through dry ingredients, leaving the shortening in small particles.

d

dough — a mixture of moistened flour with other ingredients, thick enough to be handled or kneaded.

e

f

Fattigman — a Dutch Christmas cookie having a dough high in egg yolks and flavored with cardamom and lemon rind. It is rolled paper thin; shaped into bowknots and deep fat fried.

fold — to combine a solid ingredient with a delicate substance such as beaten egg white or whipped cream without loss of air. Insert the edge of a spoon or other utensil vertically down through the middle of the mixture, slide the spoon across the bottom of the bowl, bring it up with some of the mixture and fold over on top of the rest. Continue until all is evenly mixed.

g

glaze — to coat with syrup, thin icing or jelly, either during cooking or after the food is cooked.

h

honey — a food from flower nectar, concentrated by bees. Honey contains sugars and about 20% water. Used in candy making, baking, cooking and for table use. The flavor is determined by the flavor from which the bees obtain the nectar. White clover honey is usually used in cookie baking. Buckwheat honey is frequently used as a topping for pancakes, waffles or French toast.

i

icing — a thick mixture of sugar and other ingredients, either cooked or uncooked; frosting.

j

k

kisses — small meringue-type cookies dropped on a cookie sheet to form a peak and baked in a very low oven.

knead — to work dough by repeatedly stretching it with the hands, folding it over and pressing it with the knuckles or with the "heel" of the hand.

l

m

macaroons — cookies made from egg white and sugar, usually containing almonds, ground or chopped, or almond flavoring.

meringue — a mixture of stiffly beaten egg whites and sugar sometimes having flavoring added. It is baked until lightly browned.

milk:

buttermilk — a fermented milk product from which fat has been removed in the process of churning. To sour sweet milk use I tablespoon lemon juice or vinegar plus sweet milk to make I cup.

condensed milk (sweetened) — canned whole milk from which the water has been evaporated, and to which approximately 40% sugar has been added.

dry milk (powdered milk) — the powder that remains when water is removed from whole milk. Contains at least 26% milk fat. Non-fat dry milk is the powder that results from the removal of water and butterfat from whole milk. I cup reconstituted non-fat dry milk plus 2 teaspoons butter is the equivalent of I cup whole milk.

evaporated milk — canned milk from which more than half the water has been removed. The remaining milk is homogenized and fortified with vitamin D. ½ cup evaporated milk plus ½ cup water is the equivalent of I cup whole milk.

whole milk (cow's milk) — milk that has not had the butterfat removed, and is usually pasteurized by being subjected to high temperatures to destroy certain undesirable bacteria. It is available homogenized, vitamin D fortified, condensed, evaporated or powdered.

mocha — a combination of coffee and chocolate flavors.

n

o

p

Pfeffernuesse — traditional German Christmas cookies flavored with spices and orange rind and shaped into small balls.

Pepparkakor — traditional Swedish Christmas cookies flavored with spices and frequently cut into animal shapes.

prepared lemon peel — commercially available dried grated lemon peel.

prepared orange peel — commercially available dried grated orange peel.

r

Rosettes — cookies made from a thin batter fried in deep hot fat on a specially designed rosette iron.

s

Sandbakel — traditional Swedish cookies baked in tiny Sandbakel pans or tiny tart pans.

Springerle — traditional German Christmas cookies flavored with anise, rolled and cut with a Springerle rolling pin or pressed into a Springerle mold. The cookies should be allowed to mellow in a tightly covered container for several weeks before serving.

sliver — to cut in long, thin pieces.

sugar:

confectioners' sugar — also called powdered sugar. A fine, powdery sugar made by grinding and sifting granulated sugar. Used in frostings and icings or to coat cookies.

granulated sugar — clear white crystals of purified raw sugar from which the molasses has been removed. Used in cooking, baking, and for the table. Available in various forms, such as fine, granulated, extra-fine granulated.

superfine granulated — an especially fine-grained granulated sugar used when quick dissolving is essential, as in iced drinks.

t

v

vanilla sugar — confectioners' sugar into which has been scraped the inside of a vanilla bean. It should be stored tightly covered for about one week before using to coat cookies or use in frostings.

w

whip — to beat rapidly with wire whisk or beater to add air and make a substance light and fluffy.

y

yeast — a tiny living plant which reacts with sugar to produce carbon dioxide, used as a leavening for yeast doughs.

active dry yeast — yeast and a filler of starch in a dry, granular mixture. This type of yeast can be stored at room temperature for several months.

compressed yeast — a yeast and starch mixture containing moisture. It must be refrigerated and its storage life is usually a maximum of two weeks.

Cookies For Kiddies To Make

• Youngsters love to help Mommy bake—especially cookies. Even at four boys and girls are delighted to help cut cookies with a cookie cutter and decorate them with raisins, nuts, and chocolate pieces. Their creative talents and taste in decorations may be less than artistic but it is a wonderful learning experience for them as well as keeping them occupied and they are sure to enjoy eating their "masterpieces".

Start them with simple recipes that they can help prepare. Never let young children handle sharp knives, operate the mixer or turn on the oven. Show them how to measure and get the ingredients out for them. Cut-out cookies, especially animal shapes and gingerbread men they are able to decorate, will be most appealing to the preschoolers. Drop and bar cookies will be more satisfying to the seven and eight year olds who can master a simple recipe. They will be more interested in the quantity of results rather than the appearance so they can share their goodies with their friends.

Baking Rules for Youngsters
 1. Wash your hands before starting.
 2. Put on an apron so you don't get your clothes dirty.
 3. Read the recipe directions carefully. Ask Mommy to explain anything you don't understand.
 4. Have Mommy get out all the things you'll need for the recipe.
 5. Have Mommy turn the oven on at the right temperature.
 6. Have your cookie sheets or baking pans all ready.
 7. Measure all the ingredients carefully. Be sure to fill liquids like milk just up to the line on the measuring cup. Level off the tops of dry ingredients in measuring cup or spoons with the edge of a spatula.
 8. Mix all the ingredients carefully so they are well blended. Follow the directions for putting on cookie sheets or in baking pans.
 9. Have Mommy put pans in the oven and set timer for taking them out.
 10. Clean up the dirty dishes and any spilled flour. Help put away other ingredients.
 11. Have Mommy take cookies out of oven when done and place on cooling racks.
 12. When cookies are cool, place in cookie jar or make frosting and decorate before putting away.

Ginger Cookie Capers

2 cups Pillsbury's Best All Purpose Flour
1 teaspoon baking powder
¼ teaspoon soda
1 teaspoon cinnamon
½ teaspoon ginger
⅓ cup sugar
½ cup shortening
½ cup molasses
3 tablespoons hot water

OVEN 400°   12 OR 24 COOKIES

In large mixer bowl combine all ingredients. Blend well with mixer. Chill dough at least an hour for easier handling.

Roll out dough on floured surface to ⅛-inch thickness. Cut with gingerbread man cutter. (Makes 12 6-inch or 24 4-inch gingerbread men.) Place on ungreased cookie sheets.

Bake at 400° for 8 to 10 minutes. Cool. If desired, sprinkle with additional granulated sugar or decorate.

Grandma's Caramel Cookies

3½ cups Pillsbury's Best All Purpose Flour
1 teaspoon baking powder
½ teaspoon salt
¼ teaspoon soda
1½ cups firmly packed brown sugar
½ cup shortening
½ cup butter, softened
1 egg
⅓ cup evaporated milk
1 teaspoon vanilla extract
Sugar to sprinkle

OVEN 400°   66 TO 72 COOKIES

In large mixer bowl combine all ingredients except granulated sugar. Blend well. Chill dough for easier handling.

Roll out half at a time on floured surface to ⅛-inch thickness. Cut into rounds with a 2½-inch cutter. Place on ungreased cookie sheets. Sprinkle with sugar.

Bake at 400° for 8 to 10 minutes until light golden brown.

Caramel Crisps

2 cups Pillsbury's Best All Purpose Flour
½ teaspoon salt
1 cup firmly packed brown sugar
½ cup butter, softened
⅓ cup shortening
½ cup almond paste
1 tablespoon milk
1 teaspoon almond extract
Sugar to sprinkle

OVEN 350°   60 TO 66 COOKIES

In large mixer bowl combine all ingredients except granulated sugar. Blend well.

Roll out, half at a time, on floured surface to ⅛-inch thickness. Cut into desired shapes with cookie cutters. Place on ungreased cookie sheets. Sprinkle with granulated sugar.

Bake at 350° for 8 to 10 minutes. Cool before removing from cookie sheets.

Grandma's Special Tea Cookies

2¼ cups Pillsbury's Best All Purpose Flour
½ teaspoon salt
1 cup confectioners' sugar
1 cup butter, softened
1 egg
2 teaspoons vanilla extract
½ cup chopped walnuts
2 tablespoons sugar

OVEN 400°   54 to 60 COOKIES

In large mixer bowl combine all ingredients except walnuts and granulated sugar. Blend well. Chill for easier handling.

Roll out on floured surface, half at a time, to ⅛-inch thickness. Cut into desired shapes with cookie cutter. Place on ungreased cookie sheets. Combine walnuts and granulated sugar. Sprinkle each cookie with ½ teaspoon of mixture. Bake at 400° for 8 to 10 minutes. Cool.

Grandma's
Special
Tea Cookies

Grandma's Butter Crisp

Ginger Cookie Capers

Grandma's Caramel Cookies

17

Maple
Peanut
Yummies

Chocolate Party
Dips

Crickets

Cracker Jills

Maple Peanut Yummies

1¾ cups Pillsbury's Best All Purpose Flour
½ teaspoon soda
½ teaspoon salt
¼ teaspoon baking powder
½ cup firmly packed brown sugar
½ cup shortening
½ cup crunchy peanut butter
⅓ cup maple syrup
1 egg

OVEN 350°   48 TO 54 COOKIES

In large mixer bowl combine all ingredients. Blend well with mixer.

Shape into balls using a rounded teaspoon for each. Place on ungreased cookie sheets; flatten with a fork, criss-cross fashion.

Bake at 350° for 12 to 15 minutes. Cool.
HIGH ALTITUDE ADJUSTMENT (5200 FEET)
Oven temperature 375°.

Cracker Jills

1 (3-ounce) package cream cheese
2 cups Pillsbury's Best All Purpose Flour
1¼ cups firmly packed brown sugar
½ cup butter
¼ cup molasses
½ teaspoon soda
1 egg
1 cup salted Spanish peanuts
2 cups coarsely crushed soda crackers
Sugar

OVEN 375°   54 TO 60 COOKIES

In large mixer bowl, combine all ingredients except peanuts, crackers and sugar. Blend well with mixer. Fold in peanuts and crackers; blend well. Cover; chill about 2 hours.

Shape dough into small balls, using a rounded teaspoon for each. Roll in sugar. Place on ungreased cookie sheets.

Bake at 375° for 10 to 12 minutes.

Chocolate Party Dips

⅓ cup butter
½ cup semi-sweet chocolate pieces
1 cup Pillsbury's Best All Purpose Flour
¼ teaspoon salt
¼ teaspoon soda
½ cup confectioners' sugar
1 egg
1 teaspoon vanilla extract
½ cup chopped walnuts
½ cup raisins
1½ cups plain or cocoa-flavored rice crispy cereal

OVEN 350°   36 TO 42 COOKIES

In large saucepan melt butter and chocolate pieces over low heat, stirring constantly. Remove from heat. Stir in remaining ingredients. Blend well.

Drop by teaspoon onto greased cookie sheets. Bake at 350° for 10 to 12 minutes. Cool.

Crickets

1¼ cups Pillsbury's Best All Purpose Flour
½ teaspoon salt
½ teaspoon soda
½ cup sugar
¼ cup firmly packed brown sugar
1 egg
1 teaspoon vanilla extract
½ cup butter, softened
1 cup diced toasted almonds
1 cup chocolate covered raisins

OVEN 375°   54 TO 60 COOKIES

In large mixer bowl combine all ingredients except almonds and raisins. Blend well with mixer. Stir in almonds and raisins. Drop by teaspoon 2 inches apart onto ungreased cookie sheets.

Bake at 375° for 10 to 12 minutes. Cool.

Variation: Chocolate covered peanuts may be substituted for raisins; flaked coconut may be substituted for almonds. Increase flour to 1½ cups.

Peanut Brittle Cookies

    I cup Pillsbury's Best All Purpose Flour
    ½ cup butter, softened
    ½ cup firmly packed brown sugar
    ½ teaspoon cinnamon
    ¼ teaspoon soda
    I egg
    I teaspoon vanilla extract
    I cup chopped salted peanuts

OVEN 325°   24 BARS

In large mixer bowl combine all ingredients except peanuts. Blend well. Stir in ½ cup peanuts. Spread in greased 13x9-inch pan. Sprinkle with remaining ½ cup peanuts, pressing lightly into dough.

Bake at 325° for 20 to 25 minutes. Cut into bars. Cool.

Malted Milk Date Bars

    ⅓ cup butter
    ⅔ cup Pillsbury's Best All Purpose Flour
    ½ teaspoon baking powder
    ¾ cup firmly packed brown sugar
    ¾ cup instant chocolate malted milk powder
    2 eggs
    ½ teaspoon vanilla extract
    I cup chopped dates
    ¾ cup chopped walnuts

OVEN 350°   16 BARS

Melt butter in large saucepan. Add remaining ingredients, blend well. Spread in greased 9-inch square pan. Bake at 350° for 25 to 30 minutes. Cool; cut into bars.

HIGH ALTITUDE ADJUSTMENT (5200 FEET)
Oven temperature 375°. Decrease brown sugar to ½ cup.

Chewy Butterscotch Brownies

Malted Milk Date Bars

Peanut Brittle Cookies

Corny Islands

Chocolity Poppers

Chocolate Beau Catchers

Peanut Butter Quickies

1½ cups sugar
¾ cup Pillsbury's Best All Purpose Flour
½ cup butter
½ cup milk
1½ cups quick-cooking rolled oats
⅔ cup peanut butter
½ cup chopped walnuts
½ cup flaked coconut
1 teaspoon vanilla extract
¼ teaspoon salt

54 TO 60 COOKIES

In large saucepan combine sugar, flour, butter and milk. Bring to a full boil; boil hard 3 minutes, stirring constantly.

Remove from heat; add remaining ingredients. Blend well. Drop by teaspoon onto foil or wax paper. Cool.

Coconut Balls: Drop cookies into flaked coconut; roll to coat.

Marshmallow Fudge Bars

Cherry Malted Cookies

Peanut Butter Quickies

Fudge Nut Thins

Chocodiles

21

Chocolate Beau Catchers

   2 cups Pillsbury's Best All Purpose Flour
½ teaspoon soda
½ teaspoon salt
   I cup sugar
¾ cup butter, softened
½ cup milk
   2 (I ounce) envelopes premelted
     unsweetened chocolate
   I egg
   I teaspoon vanilla extract
1¼ cups (8-ounce package) chopped dates
½ cup chopped walnuts

OVEN 350°   54 TO 60 COOKIES

In large mixer bowl combine all ingredients for cookies except dates and walnuts. Blend well with mixer. Stir in remaining ingredients.

Drop by rounded teaspoon onto ungreased cookie sheets. Bake at 350° for 10 to 12 minutes. Cool. Frost.

Vanilla Frosting

Prepare I package (small size) Pillsbury Buttercream Vanilla Frosting Mix as directed on package.

Marshmallow Fudge Bars

½ cup shortening
¾ cup Pillsbury's Best All Purpose Flour
¼ teaspoon baking powder
¼ teaspoon salt
¾ cup sugar
   2 tablespoons cocoa
   2 eggs
   I teaspoon vanilla extract
½ cup chopped pecans

OVEN 350°   18 BARS

In large saucepan melt shortening over low heat. Remove from heat. Add remaining ingredients. Blend well. Spread in greased 9-inch square pan.

Bake at 350° for 25 to 30 minutes. Cool and frost. Cut into bars.

Rocky Road Frosting

Prepare I package (small size) Pillsbury Buttercream Fudge Frosting Mix as directed on package. Stir in ½ cup miniature marshmallows.

Fudge Nut Thins

½ cup butter
   2 (I-ounce) envelopes premelted
     unsweetened chocolate
¾ cup Pillsbury's Best All Purpose Flour
   I teaspoon baking powder
¼ teaspoon salt
   I cup sugar
   2 eggs
½ teaspoon vanilla extract
   I cup chopped walnuts

OVEN 350°   36 BARS

In large saucepan melt butter and chocolate over low heat, stirring constantly. Remove from heat. Add remaining ingredients except walnuts. Blend well. Stir in ½ cup walnuts.

Spread in greased 15x10x1-inch jelly roll pan. Bake at 350° for 12 to 15 minutes. Cool. Frost, then sprinkle with ½ cup walnuts. Cut in bars.

Fudge-Almond Frosting

Prepare I package (small size) Pillsbury Buttercream Fudge Frosting Mix as directed on package, adding ½ teaspoon almond extract to water.
HIGH ALTITUDE ADJUSTMENT (5200 FEET)
Oven temperature 375°. Decrease butter to ⅓ cup.

Chocolity Poppers

½ cup butter
   I (10½-ounce) package miniature
     marshmallows
   2 (I-ounce) squares semi-sweet chocolate
   I cup Pillsbury's Best All Purpose Flour
   I teaspoon vanilla extract
   I cup salted peanuts
   6 cups popcorn

OVEN 350°   36 BARS

In 2-quart saucepan combine butter, marshmallows and chocolate. Cook over low heat, stirring constantly, until melted and well blended. Remove from heat. Gradually add flour and salt, mixing well. Stir in vanilla extract and peanuts. Pour over popcorn, mixing well. Press into well-greased 13x9-inch pan.

Bake at 350° for 10 to 12 minutes. Cool; cut into bars. Dust with confectioners' sugar, if desired.

Tip: Unsweetened chocolate may be substituted for semi-sweet; add 2 tablespoons sugar.

Chewy Butterscotch Brownies

¾ cup butter
1½ cups firmly packed brown sugar
1 cup flaked coconut
¾ cup butterscotch pieces
1¾ cups Pillsbury's Best All Purpose Flour
½ teaspoon soda
¼ teaspoon salt
½ teaspoon vanilla extract
1 egg
1 cup miniature marshmallows
½ cup chopped pecans

OVEN 350°   48 BARS

In medium saucepan melt ¼ cup butter. Stir in ½ cup brown sugar, coconut and butterscotch pieces. Spread in bottom of greased 13x9-inch pan.

In large mixer bowl combine ½ cup butter, 1 cup brown sugar and remaining ingredients except marshmallows and pecans. Blend well with mixer. Fold in marshmallows and pecans. Spoon dough in small amounts over coconut mixture; pat out evenly.
Bake at 350° for 25 to 30 minutes. While warm drizzle with Butterscotch Glaze. Cut into bars.

Butterscotch Glaze

1 tablespoon butter
1 tablespoon light corn syrup
¼ cup butterscotch pieces
1 cup confectioners' sugar
2 to 3 tablespoons milk

Melt butter, corn syrup and butterscotch pieces over low heat, stirring constantly. Remove from heat. Add confectioners' sugar and milk until consistency of a glaze.

Corny Islands

1 package Pillsbury Fluffy White Frosting Mix
¼ teaspoon maple extract
½ cup Pillsbury's Best All Purpose Flour
1 teaspoon baking powder
3 cups caramel corn
½ cup butterscotch pieces
½ cup salted Spanish peanuts

OVEN 325°   36 COOKIES

Prepare frosting mix as directed on package, adding maple extract with water. Fold in flour and baking powder. In large mixing bowl combine remaining ingredients. Add frosting mixture, mixing well. Drop by tablespoon onto greased and floured cookie sheets.
Bake at 325° for 20 to 25 minutes. Cool slightly; remove from cookie sheets.
Variation: Semi-sweet chocolate pieces may be substituted for butterscotch; salted cashews may be substituted for Spanish peanuts.

Chocodiles

2½ cups Pillsbury's Best All Purpose Flour
1¼ cups firmly packed brown sugar
½ cup butter, softened
½ cup shortening
½ teaspoon salt
⅓ cup crunchy peanut butter
1 egg
1 teaspoon vanilla extract

OVEN 350°   36 BARS

In large mixer bowl combine all ingredients. Blend with mixer to form a dough. Press in ungreased 15x10x1-inch jelly roll pan.
Bake at 350° for 20 to 25 minutes. Cool slightly. Spread with Chocolate Crunch. While warm, cut into bars.

Chocolate Crunch

Melt 1 cup (6-ounce package) semi-sweet chocolate pieces in medium saucepan. Stir in ½ cup crunchy peanut butter and 1½ cups slightly crushed corn flakes.

Cherry Malted Cookies

1½ cups Pillsbury's Best All Purpose Flour
⅔ cup firmly packed brown sugar
½ cup instant chocolate malted milk powder
½ teaspoon cinnamon
½ teaspoon salt
¼ teaspoon soda
1 egg
½ cup shortening
2 tablespoons maraschino cherry juice
1 teaspoon vanilla extract
¼ cup chopped maraschino cherries, drained

OVEN 375°   30 TO 36 COOKIES

In large mixer bowl combine all ingredients except cherries. Blend well with mixer. Stir in cherries; mix thoroughly.
Drop by rounded teaspoon onto ungreased cookie sheets. Bake at 375° for 12 to 15 minutes. Cool.

Cookie Jar Cookies

• Get set for that attack by the after school raiders on the cookie jar. Active boys and girls have bottomless appetites and cookies are a nourishing and filling "energy break" to keep them going till dinner time.

Maybe both youngsters and oldsters in your family are TV munchers who enjoy nibbling their way through their favorite program. Please them all with an assortment of their favorite cookies in a conveniently placed cookie jar.

Nighttime cookie snitchers are notorious for their before bedtime forays on the cookie jar. With a glass of milk this can be a nutritious and sleep promoting snack.

Lucky for you, all of these recipes are quick and easy to make in order to keep the cookie jar well filled with everyone's favorites.

Almond Butter Sticks

    I cup butter, softened
    I (8-ounce) package cream cheese,
      softened
2¼ cups Pillsbury's Best All Purpose Flour
    2 teaspoons baking powder
    ⅛ teaspoon salt
  I½ cups sugar
  4½ teaspoons almond extract

OVEN 400°   60 COOKIES

In large mixing bowl combine all ingredients except sugar and almond extract. Blend with mixer until a dough forms. Knead on floured surface until smooth.

Roll out dough, half at a time, to 14x8-inch rectangles. Combine sugar and almond extract. Sprinkle each rectangle with 3 to 4 tablespoons sugar mixture.

For each rectangle fold one end of dough over center. Fold other end over to make 3 layers. Turning dough one quarter way around, repeat rolling and folding 2 more times, sprinkling with 3 to 4 tablespoons sugar mixture each time. Roll out again to 14x8-inch rectangles. Cut into 3x1½-inch strips. Place on ungreased cookie sheets.

Bake at 400° for 8 to 10 minutes. Remove from cookie sheets immediately. Cool.
HIGH ALTITUDE ADJUSTMENT (5200 FEET)
Oven temperature 425°. Decrease butter to ¾ cup and baking powder to 1½ teaspoons.

Cashew Crunch Cookies

2¼ cups Pillsbury's Best All Purpose Flour
  ½ teaspoon soda
  ½ teaspoon cream of tartar
  ¾ cup firmly packed brown sugar
  ½ cup sugar
    I cup butter, softened
    I egg
    I teaspoon vanilla extract
  I½ cups finely chopped cashews

OVEN 350°   70 TO 76 COOKIES

In large mixer bowl combine all ingredients except cashews. Blend well with mixer. Stir in cashews; mix thoroughly.

Drop by rounded teaspoon onto lightly greased cookie sheets.

Bake at 350° for 12 to 15 minutes until golden brown.

Chocolate Shadows

  ½ cup semi-sweet chocolate pieces
  ⅛ to ¼ teaspoon peppermint extract
I¼ cups Pillsbury's Best All Purpose Flour
  ¾ teaspoon soda
  ½ teaspoon salt
  ½ cup sugar
  ½ cup firmly packed brown sugar
  ½ cup shortening
  ½ cup peanut butter
    I egg

OVEN 375°   42 TO 48 COOKIES

In a small saucepan melt chocolate pieces over low heat stirring constantly. Remove from heat. Stir in peppermint extract. Set aside and cool.

In a large mixer bowl combine remaining ingredients. Blend well with mixer. Add melted chocolate and *stir just to revel.*

Shape into balls, using a rounded teaspoon of dough for each. Place on ungreased cookie sheets. Flatten with bottom of glass which has been greased and dipped in sugar.

Bake at 375° for 8 to 10 minutes. Cool.
HIGH ALTITUDE ADJUSTMENT (5200 FEET)
Decrease soda to ½ teaspoon.

Cashew Crunch Cookies

Chocolate Shadows

Almond
Butter Sticks

27

Maple Memory Cookies

2¼ cups Pillsbury's Best All Purpose Flour
2 teaspoons baking powder
½ teaspoon soda
½ teaspoon salt
½ cup firmly packed brown sugar
¾ cup shortening
1 egg
½ cup maple syrup
1 teaspoon maple flavoring
½ cup chopped walnuts

OVEN 400°   36 TO 42 COOKIES

In large mixer bowl combine all ingredients except walnuts. Blend well with mixer. Stir in walnuts; mix thoroughly.

Drop by rounded teaspoon onto ungreased cookie sheets. If desired top each with a walnut half.

Bake at 400° for 8 to 10 minutes. Cool.
*HIGH ALTITUDE ADJUSTMENT (5200 FEET)
Decrease baking powder to 1 teaspoon.*

Chocolate Peanut Cookies

Chocolate Dough:
1 cup Pillsbury's Best All Purpose Flour
¾ cup sugar
1 teaspoon salt
½ cup shortening
1 egg
2 (1-ounce) envelopes premelted unsweetened chocolate
1 teaspoon vanilla extract

Peanut Butter Dough:
2 tablespoons Pillsbury's Best All Purpose Flour
½ cup firmly packed brown sugar
¼ cup creamy peanut butter
2 tablespoons butter, softened

OVEN 325°   36 TO 42 COOKIES

In large mixer bowl combine all ingredients for Chocolate Dough. Blend well with mixer. Set aside.

In small mixer bowl combine all ingredients for Peanut Butter Dough. Blend well with mixer.

Spoon level teaspoon of Chocolate Dough and then a scant ½ teaspoon of Peanut Butter Dough. Drop onto ungreased cookie sheets. Press with a fork dipped in flour.

Bake at 325° for 12 to 15 minutes. Cool 1 minute. Remove from cookie sheet. Cookie is very tender.

Maple-Scotch Snaps

2¼ cups Pillsbury's Best All Purpose Flour
2 cups firmly packed brown sugar
½ cup butter, softened
1 teaspoon soda
½ teaspoon salt
2 tablespoons milk
1 egg
1 teaspoon maple flavoring
½ cup chopped pecans
2 tablespoons instant chocolate
   beverage mix

OVEN 375°   60 TO 66 COOKIES

In large mixer bowl combine flour, brown sugar and butter. Blend with mixer until particles are fine. Reserve ¼ cup for topping.

Add remaining ingredients except chocolate beverage mix and mix thoroughly.

Shape into balls, using a rounded teaspoon for each. Combine reserved crumbs and beverage mix. Roll balls in chocolate-sugar mixture. Place on ungreased cookie sheets.

Bake at 375° for 12 to 15 minutes. Cookies will puff and collapse during baking.

Cherry-Chocolate Honeys

2 cups Pillsbury's Best All Purpose Flour
1 teaspoon soda
1 teaspoon salt
1 cup shortening
1 teaspoon vanilla extract
¾ cup honey
1 cup quick-cooking rolled oats
½ cup chopped filberts
½ cup semi-sweet chocolate pieces
¼ cup chopped maraschino cherries,
   drained

OVEN 375°   42 TO 48 COOKIES

In large mixer bowl combine all ingredients except oats, filberts, chocolate pieces and cherries. Blend well. Stir in remaining ingredients. Mix thoroughly.

Drop by rounded teaspoon onto ungreased cookie sheets. Bake at 375° for 10 to 12 minutes. Cool.

Oatmeal Chip Cookies

Butter Pecan Crunchers

Oatmeal Chip Cookies

2 cups Pillsbury's Best All Purpose Flour
1 teaspoon salt
1 teaspoon soda
1 cup sugar
1 cup firmly packed brown sugar
½ cup butter, softened
½ cup shortening
2 eggs
2 cups quick-cooking rolled oats
1 cup chopped almonds
1 cup (6-ounce package) semi-sweet
chocolate pieces

OVEN 375°   90 TO 96 COOKIES

In large mixer bowl combine all ingredients except oats, almonds and chocolate pieces. Blend well with mixer. Stir in remaining ingredients; mix thoroughly. If desired, chill dough for easier handling.

Shape into balls, using a rounded teaspoon for each. Place on ungreased cookie sheets. Bake at 375° for 10 to 12 minutes. Cool.

Butter Pecan Crunchers

2 tablespoons plus ½ cup butter, softened
1¾ cups firmly packed brown sugar
1 cup chopped pecans
2 cups Pillsbury's Best All Purpose Flour
½ teaspoon baking powder
1 egg
1 teaspoon rum flavoring
½ teaspoon vanilla extract

OVEN 375°   48 TO 54 COOKIES

Combine 2 tablespoons butter, ½ cup brown sugar and pecans. Mix until just blended together. Set aside.

In large mixer bowl combine ½ cup butter, 1¼ cups brown sugar and remaining ingredients. Blend well with mixer. Stir in pecan mixture just until evenly distributed.

Shape into balls, using a rounded teaspoon for each. Place on ungreased cookie sheet; flatten slightly with bottom of glass greased and dipped in flour.

Bake at 375° for 10 to 12 minutes. Cool slightly before removing from cookie sheet.

Cherry Pom-Poms

    I cup Pillsbury's Best All Purpose Flour
½ teaspoon baking powder
½ cup cooking oil
  3 tablespoons cherry-flavored gelatin
  I (3¾-ounce) package instant vanilla
    pudding mix
  2 eggs, separated
  3 tablespoons milk
½ teaspoon almond extract
¾ cup chopped pecans
  I (7-ounce) package flaked coconut
  I teaspoon water

OVEN 350°   36 TO 42 COOKIES

In large mixer bowl combine all ingredients except pecans, coconut, egg whites and water. Blend well with mixer. Stir in pecans and ⅔ cup coconut.

Shape into balls, using a rounded teaspoon for each. Slightly beat egg whites with water. Roll balls in egg whites, then in remaining coconut. Place on ungreased cookie sheets, pressing down to flatten. Bake at 350° for 15 to 18 minutes or until delicately browned.

Coconut Cherry Drops

  I¼ cups Pillsbury's Best All Purpose Flour
½ teaspoon baking powder
½ teaspoon salt
½ cup butter, softened
½ cup sugar
½ teaspoon almond extract
  I egg
  I cup flaked coconut
½ cup chopped pecans
¼ cup chopped maraschino cherries,
    drained

OVEN 375°   30 TO 36 COOKIES

In large mixer bowl combine all ingredients except coconut, pecans and cherries. Blend well with mixer. Stir in remaining ingredients; mix thoroughly.

Drop by rounded teaspoon onto greased cookie sheets. Bake at 375° for 10 to 12 minutes. Cool.

Twin Cinnamon Whirls

2¼ cups Pillsbury's Best All Purpose Flour
  2 teaspoons baking powder
  I teaspoon salt
  I cup sugar
 ½ cup butter, softened
  I cup creamed cottage cheese
  I egg
  I teaspoon vanilla extract
  2 teaspoons cinnamon
  3 tablespoons butter, melted

OVEN 350°   48 COOKIES

In large mixer bowl combine all ingredients except ¾ cup sugar, cinnamon and melted butter. Blend well with mixer. Chill at least 2 hours.

Combine remaining sugar and cinnamon. Divide dough into 3 balls. Roll out I portion to a 12-inch circle on surface sprinkled with ¼ cup cinnamon-sugar. Turn dough over several times to coat with cinnamon-sugar. Brush with I tablespoon melted butter. Cut into 16 wedges. Roll up, starting with wide end and roll to point.

Place on ungreased cookie sheets. Cut one-half of the way through center of wedge. Spread apart. Repeat with remaining dough.

Bake at 350° for 20 to 25 minutes. Serve warm or cold.

Long Ago Lemon Cookies

¼ cup butter
2¼ cups Pillsbury's Best All Purpose Flour
I teaspoon soda
I teaspoon salt
1⅓ cups plus ¼ cup sugar
1½ teaspoons prepared lemon peel
2 cups dairy sour cream
¼ teaspoon mace or nutmeg

OVEN 375°   42 TO 48 COOKIES

In large saucepan melt butter over low heat. Remove from heat. Add remaining ingredients except ¼ cup sugar and mace. Blend well.

Drop by well-rounded teaspoon onto ungreased cookie sheets. Sprinkle with mixture of remaining sugar and mace.

Bake at 375° for 10 to 15 minutes until very lightly browned. Cool.

Milk Chocolate Crunchies

I cup butter, softened
½ cup shortening
I package (regular size) Pillsbury Buttercream Vanilla Frosting Mix
2¼ cups Pillsbury's Best All Purpose Flour
½ teaspoon salt
2 cups finely chopped walnuts
I (9¾-ounce) milk chocolate bar, melted

OVEN 325°   66 TO 72 COOKIES

In large mixer bowl, combine all ingredients except nuts and chocolate. Blend well with mixer. Stir in nuts and chocolate.

Shape into 1¼-inch balls. Place on ungreased cookie sheets. Bake at 325° for 12 to 15 minutes. Cool before removing from cookie sheets.

Tip: If desired, substitute Pillsbury Buttercream Fudge or Milk Chocolate Frosting Mix.

Swedish Oatmeal Cookies

Cookie Dough:
¾ cup Pillsbury's Best All Purpose Flour
½ teaspoon soda
½ teaspoon salt
½ cup sugar
½ cup firmly packed brown sugar
½ cup shortening
I egg
½ teaspoon vanilla extract
1½ cups quick-cooking rolled oats

Almond Topping:
⅓ cup sugar
¼ cup butter
I tablespoon light corn syrup
⅓ cup chopped slivered almonds
⅛ teaspoon almond extract

OVEN 350°   35 TO 40 COOKIES

In large mixer bowl combine all cookie ingredients except rolled oats. Blend well with mixer. Stir in rolled oats.

Drop by rounded teaspoon onto ungreased cookie sheets. Bake at 350° for 8 minutes. Remove from oven and place a scant ½ teaspoon Almond Topping in center of each cookie, pressing in slightly.

Bake at 350° for 6 to 8 minutes until cookies are golden brown. Cool I minute before removing from cookie sheet.

Topping: Combine sugar, butter and corn syrup in a saucepan; bring to a boil. Remove from heat. Stir in almonds and almond extract.
*HIGH ALTITUDE ADJUSTMENT (5200 FEET)
Oven temperature 375°.*

Orange-Oatmeal Chews

    I cup quick-cooking rolled oats
¾ cup Pillsbury's Best All Purpose Flour
    I teaspoon salt
½ teaspoon baking powder
½ teaspoon soda
½ cup sugar
½ cup firmly packed brown sugar
½ cup shortening
    I egg
    I teaspoon vanilla extract
    2 tablespoons prepared orange peel
½ cup chopped walnuts

OVEN 350°   34 TO 40 COOKIES

Toast rolled oats in a shallow pan at 350° for 10 to 12 minutes. Cool.

In large mixer bowl combine remaining ingredients except walnuts. Blend well with mixer. Stir in the toasted rolled oats and walnuts.

Drop by rounded teaspoon onto ungreased cookie sheets.

Bake at 350° for 10 to 12 minutes until golden brown. Cool 1 minute; remove from cookie sheet.

Orange Raisin Drops

    2 cups Pillsbury's Best All Purpose Flour
    I teaspoon soda
½ teaspoon salt
    I teaspoon cinnamon
    I teaspoon nutmeg
    I cup firmly packed brown sugar
    I tablespoon prepared orange peel
¾ cup shortening
    2 eggs
    2 tablespoons milk
    I cup quick-cooking rolled oats
    I cup raisins
½ cup chopped walnuts

OVEN 375°   48 TO 54 COOKIES

In large mixer bowl combine all ingredients except rolled oats, raisins and walnuts. Blend well with mixer. Stir in remaining ingredients; mix thoroughly.

Drop by rounded teaspoon onto greased cookie sheets. Flatten slightly with a fork.

Bake at 375° for 10 to 12 minutes. Cool.

Chocolate Nutbutter Cookies

    2 cups Pillsbury's Best All Purpose Flour
    2 teaspoons baking powder
½ teaspoon salt
1¼ cups sugar
½ cup cocoa
½ cup shortening
½ cup crunchy peanut butter
⅓ cup milk
    2 eggs
1½ teaspoons vanilla extract

OVEN 400°   54 TO 60 COOKIES

In large mixer bowl combine all ingredients. Blend well with mixer. If desired, chill dough for easier handling.

Shape dough into balls, using a rounded teaspoon for each. Place on ungreased cookie sheets. Flatten with fork, criss-cross fashion.

Bake at 400° for 8 to 10 minutes. Do not overbake. This is a soft cookie.

Orange Sparkle Cookies

2¼ cups Pillsbury's Best All Purpose Flour
    I teaspoon soda
½ teaspoon salt
    I cup sugar
¾ cup butter, softened
    I egg
¼ cup orange juice
    2 tablespoons prepared orange peel
    I teaspoon lemon extract
    I teaspoon orange extract
½ cup chopped walnuts
    Sugar to sprinkle

OVEN 350°   50 TO 56 COOKIES

In large mixer bowl combine all ingredients except walnuts and sugar to sprinkle. Blend well with mixer. Stir in walnuts; mix thoroughly. Chill 1 to 2 hours.

Drop by teaspoon onto ungreased cookie sheets. Sprinkle with sugar. Bake at 350° for 12 to 15 minutes until light golden brown. Cool.

HIGH ALTITUDE ADJUSTMENT (5200 FEET)
Oven temperature 375°.

Long Ago Lemon Cookies

Orange-Oatmeal Chews

Milk Chocolate Crunchies

Swedish Oatmeal Cookies

Orange Raisin Drops

Orange Sparkle Cook

36

Toffee Nut Cookies

Java Crunch Cookies

colate Munchers

colate Nutbutter Cookies

Toffee Topper Cookies

Double Crunchers

Roll-in-Sugar Cookies

Chewy Date Drops

Roll-in-Sugar Cookies

I package active dry yeast
½ cup warm water
I cup butter, softened
2¼ cups Pillsbury's Best All Purpose Flour
I tablespoon vanilla extract
½ cup sugar
½ cup finely chopped pecans

OVEN 375°   42 TO 48 COOKIES

Soften yeast in water. In large mixer bowl combine butter, flour, yeast and vanilla extract. Blend well with mixer.

Shape into balls, using a rounded teaspoon for each. Combine sugar and pecans. Roll cookie balls in sugar-nut mixture.

Place on greased cookie sheets. Let rise in warm place for 15 minutes. Bake at 375° for 20 to 25 minutes.

Toffee Topper Cookies

2 cups Pillsbury's Best All Purpose Flour
I teaspoon soda
½ teaspoon salt
I cup firmly packed brown sugar
¼ cup sugar
¾ cup butter, softened
I egg
1½ teaspoons vanilla extract
4 (¾-ounce) English toffee bars, crushed

OVEN 400°   54 TO 60 COOKIES

In large mixer bowl combine all ingredients except toffee candy. Blend well with mixer.

Shape into balls, using a teaspoon for each. Place 3 inches apart on ungreased cookie sheets. Flatten with bottom of glass dipped in sugar. Cover center of cookie with about ½ teaspoon of crushed candy.

Bake at 400° for 8 to 10 minutes. Cool.

Chewy Date Drops

2 cups chopped dates
1½ cups sugar
½ cup water
4 cups Pillsbury's Best All Purpose Flour
I teaspoon soda
I teaspoon salt
I cup butter, softened
I cup firmly packed brown sugar
I teaspoon vanilla extract
3 eggs
I cup chopped walnuts

OVEN 375°   80 TO 86 COOKIES

In medium saucepan combine dates, ½ cup sugar and water. Cook over low heat, stirring occasionally, until thickened. Cool.

In large mixer bowl combine I cup sugar and remaining ingredients except walnuts. Blend well with mixer. Stir in date mixture and walnuts. Mix thoroughly.

Drop by rounded teaspoon onto greased cookie sheets. Bake at 375° for 12 to 15 minutes. Cool.

Double Crunchers

I cup Pillsbury's Best All Purpose Flour
½ teaspoon soda
¼ teaspoon salt
½ cup firmly packed brown sugar
½ cup sugar
½ cup shortening
I egg
½ teaspoon vanilla extract
I cup slightly crushed corn flakes
I cup quick-cooking rolled oats
½ cup flaked coconut

OVEN 350°   42 TO 48 COOKIES

In large mixer bowl combine all ingredients except corn flakes, rolled oats and coconut. Blend well with mixer. Stir in remaining ingredients; mix thoroughly.

Shape into balls using a rounded teaspoon for each. Place on ungreased cookie sheets. Flatten with bottom of a glass.

Bake at 350° for 8 to 10 minutes. Cool.

Chocolate Munchers

½ cup semi-sweet chocolate pieces
½ cup miniature marshmallows
  I tablespoon water
¾ cup Pillsbury's Best All Purpose Flour
½ cup sugar
½ teaspoon salt
½ teaspoon soda
⅓ cup firmly packed brown sugar
½ cup shortening
  I egg
  2 teaspoons almond extract
½ teaspoon vanilla extract
1¼ cups quick-cooking rolled oats
  I cup chopped pecans

OVEN 350°   42 TO 48 COOKIES

In large saucepan melt chocolate pieces, marshmallows and water over low heat, stirring constantly. Remove from heat. Add remaining ingredients except oats and pecans. Blend well. Stir in oats and pecans. Mix thoroughly.

Drop by rounded teaspoon onto ungreased cookie sheets. Bake at 350° for 12 to 15 minutes. Cool.
HIGH ALTITUDE ADJUSTMENT (5200 FEET)
Oven temperature 375°.

Toffee Nut Cookies

1¾ cups Pillsbury's Best All Purpose Flour
½ teaspoon baking powder
½ teaspoon salt
¼ teaspoon soda
  I cup firmly packed brown sugar
½ cup shortening
  2 tablespoons milk
  I egg
  I teaspoon vanilla extract
  4 (¾-ounce) English toffee bars, crushed

OVEN 375°   48 TO 54 COOKIES

In large mixer bowl combine all ingredients. Blend well with mixer.

Drop by rounded teaspoon onto greased cookie sheets.

Bake at 375° for 10 to 12 minutes.

Java Crunch Cookies

1½ cups Pillsbury's Best All Purpose Flour
  I teaspoon baking powder
½ teaspoon salt
½ cup sugar
¼ cup firmly packed brown sugar
  I tablespoon instant coffee
¾ cup butter, softened
  I egg
1½ cups flaked coconut

OVEN 350°   36 TO 42 COOKIES

In large mixer bowl combine all ingredients except coconut. Blend well with mixer. Stir in coconut; mix thoroughly.

Drop by rounded teaspoon onto ungreased cookie sheets.

Bake at 350° for 10 to 12 minutes. Cool.

Coco-runes

> 2 cups Pillsbury's Best All Purpose Flour
> I teaspoon salt
> ½ teaspoon soda
> ½ cup sugar
> ½ cup firmly packed brown sugar
> ¾ cup shortening
> I egg
> I teaspoon vanilla extract
> I cup chopped cooked prunes, drained
> Grated coconut

OVEN 350°   36 TO 42 COOKIES

In large mixer bowl combine all ingredients except prunes and coconut. Blend well with mixer. Stir in prunes; mix thoroughly.

Drop by rounded teaspoon onto greased cookie sheets. Sprinkle coconut over top of cookie.

Bake at 350° for I5 to I8 minutes. Cool.

Peanut Brittle Crispies

> I¼ cups Pillsbury's Best All Purpose Flour
> ½ teaspoon soda
> ¼ teaspoon salt
> ¼ cup sugar
> ¼ cup butter, softened
> ¼ cup shortening
> I egg
> I cup finely crushed peanut brittle

OVEN 375°   30 TO 36 COOKIES

In large mixer bowl combine all ingredients except peanut brittle. Blend well. Stir in peanut brittle; mix thoroughly.

Shape dough by rounded teaspoon into balls. Place on ungreased cookie sheets.

Bake at 375° for 8 to I0 minutes. Cool I minute before removing from cookie sheet.

Triplets

2½ cups Pillsbury's Best All Purpose Flour
2 teaspoons baking powder
1 teaspoon salt
½ cup sugar
½ cup firmly packed brown sugar
1 cup shortening
2 eggs
1 teaspoon vanilla extract
½ cup milk
1 teaspoon cinnamon
½ cup chopped dates
1 teaspoon almond extract
1 (1-ounce) envelope premelted
  unsweetened chocolate
½ cup flaked coconut

OVEN 400°   48 TO 54 COOKIES

In large mixer bowl combine all ingredients except cinnamon, dates, almond extract, chocolate and coconut. Blend well with mixer. Divide dough into 3 parts.

Add cinnamon and dates to first part. Blend almond extract into second part. Add chocolate and coconut to third part.

Dip teaspoon into first mixture, then second and third until the three flavors make up one rounded teaspoon of dough. Drop onto greased cookie sheets.

Bake at 400° for 10 to 12 minutes. Cool.

Snack Time Molasses Cookie

1½ cups Pillsbury's Best All Purpose Flour
¾ teaspoon soda
½ teaspoon salt
¾ cup sugar
½ cup shortening
¼ cup molasses
1 egg
½ cup flaked coconut
½ cup chopped walnuts

OVEN 375°   36 TO 42 COOKIES

In large mixer bowl combine all ingredients except coconut and walnuts. Blend well with mixer. Stir in remaining ingredients; mix thoroughly.

Drop by rounded teaspoon onto greased cookie sheets. Bake at 375° for 8 to 10 minutes. Cool 1 minute; remove from cookie sheet.

Old Time Fruit Drops

½ cup raisins
½ cup chopped dates
½ cup chopped walnuts
 I cup hot apricot nectar
2½ cups Pillsbury's Best All Purpose Flour
 I teaspoon baking powder
 I teaspoon soda
 I teaspoon salt
 I cup sugar
½ cup shortening
 I egg
 I tablespoon prepared orange peel
 I teaspoon vanilla extract
½ teaspoon almond extract

OVEN 400°   45 TO 50 COOKIES

Add raisins, dates and walnuts to hot apricot nectar. Set aside.

In large mixer bowl combine remaining ingredients. Blend well with mixer. Stir in the fruit and nut mixture; mix thoroughly.

Drop by rounded teaspoon onto greased cookie sheets. Bake at 400° for 10 to 12 minutes. Frost while warm with Apricot Glaze.

Apricot Glaze

Blend 2 tablespoons butter with 1½ cups confectioners' sugar. Add I tablespoon prepared orange peel and 2 to 3 tablespoons apricot nectar until the consistency of a glaze.

Caramel Oatmeal Brownies

Crumb Crust:
⅓ cup butter
½ cup firmly packed brown sugar
⅓ cup Pillsbury's Best All Purpose Flour
¼ teaspoon soda
¼ teaspoon salt
 I cup quick-cooking rolled oats

Topping:
¼ cup butter
 I (I-ounce) envelope premelted
  unsweetened chocolate
¾ cup sugar
⅔ cup Pillsbury's Best All Purpose Flour
¼ teaspoon salt
¼ teaspoon soda
 I egg
 2 tablespoons milk
 I teaspoon vanilla extract

OVEN 350°   18 BARS

To prepare crumb crust, melt butter in medium saucepan. Remove from heat, add remaining ingredients and blend until mixture forms coarse crumbs. Press in ungreased 8-inch square pan.

To prepare topping, melt butter and chocolate in same saucepan. Remove from heat. Add remaining ingredients and blend well.

Pour slowly over crumb crust. Bake at 350° for 30 to 35 minutes. Cool; cut into bars.
HIGH ALTITUDE ADJUSTMENT (5200 FEET)
Oven temperature 375°.

Scottish Reels

 2 cups Pillsbury's Best All Purpose Flour
 I teaspoon baking powder
½ teaspoon soda
½ teaspoon salt
 I cup firmly packed brown sugar
½ cup confectioners' sugar
½ cup butter, softened
½ cup shortening
 3 tablespoons (1½-ounces) cream cheese,
  softened
 2 eggs
 2 (I-ounce) envelopes premelted
  unsweetened chocolate
 2 teaspoons vanilla extract
 I cup chopped pecans
⅓ cup quick-cooking rolled oats
 2 tablespoons confectioners' sugar

OVEN 350°   60 COOKIES

In large mixer bowl combine all ingredients except pecans, oats and sugar. Blend well. Stir in pecans; mix thoroughly. Chill at least I hour.

Combine rolled oats and sugar in a small bowl.

Drop dough by rounded teaspoon onto greased cookie sheets. Flatten to about ¼ inch with glass greased on the bottom and dipped in the oat and sugar mixture.

Bake at 350° for 12 to 15 minutes. Cool; frost with Fudge Frosting.

Fudge Frosting

Prepare I package (small size) Pillsbury Buttercream Fudge Frosting Mix substituting 3 tablespoons (1½-ounces) cream cheese for butter in basic recipe.
HIGH ALTITUDE ADJUSTMENT (5200 FEET)
Oven temperature 375°. Decrease baking powder to ¾ teaspoon.

Scottish Reels

Heavenly Honey Bars

Coco-nutty Brownies

Spicy Butter Thins

Buttercream Drops

TV Munchers

Golden Nut Drops

Spell-Binders

Vernie's Date-Nut Bars

Caramel Oatmeal Brownies

Old Time Fruit Drops

Vernie's Date-Nut Bars

1 cup chopped dates
¾ cup hot water
1½ cups Pillsbury's Best All Purpose Flour
1¼ cups sugar
½ teaspoon soda
½ teaspoon salt
1 tablespoon cocoa
½ cup shortening
2 eggs
1 cup chopped pecans
Confectioners' sugar

OVEN 350°   24 BARS

Combine dates and water in small bowl. Let stand 10 minutes.
In large mixer bowl combine remaining ingredients except pecans and confectioners' sugar. Blend well with mixer. Add date mixture and pecans. Mix thoroughly. Spread in greased 13x9-inch pan.
Bake at 350° for 30 to 35 minutes. While warm, sprinkle with confectioners' sugar. Cut into bars.
HIGH ALTITUDE ADJUSTMENT (5200 FEET)
Oven temperature 375°.

TV Munchers

¾ cup butter, softened
1 package (regular size) Pillsbury Buttercream Caramel Frosting Mix
1 egg
1 cup (2 or 3) mashed ripe bananas
2 cups Pillsbury's Best All Purpose Flour
1 teaspoon baking powder
½ teaspoon soda
½ teaspoon salt
1 teaspoon cinnamon
1 cup quick-cooking rolled oats
1 cup (6-ounce package) semi-sweet chocolate pieces
Pecan halves

OVEN 375°   54 TO 60 COOKIES

In large mixer bowl combine butter, 1½ cups firmly packed dry frosting mix and remaining ingredients except pecan halves. Blend well with mixer.
Drop dough by scant tablespoon onto ungreased cookie sheets. Bake at 375° for 12 to 15 minutes. Remove from cookie sheets immediately. Cool; frost. Top each with a pecan half.

Frosting

Combine remaining dry frosting mix, 2 tablespoons butter, melted, and 2 to 3 tablespoons light cream; blend well.
Tip: Two (4¾-ounce) jars banana baby food may be substituted for the mashed bananas.

Buttercream Drops

1 cup butter
1 cup evaporated milk
1 cup Pillsbury's Best All Purpose Flour
1 package (regular size) Pillsbury Buttercream Milk Chocolate Frosting Mix
2 cups chopped walnuts
4 to 5 cups dry cereal flakes or pieces

54 TO 60 COOKIES

Melt butter in heavy 3-quart saucepan over medium heat. Remove from heat. Stir in milk, flour and dry frosting mix; blend until smooth. Cook over medium heat, stirring constantly, until mixture thickens and leaves sides of pan, about 15 minutes. Remove from heat. Stir in walnuts and cereal. Drop by tablespoon onto waxed paper, foil or Teflon-coated cookie sheet.
Tip: Your favorite flavor of Pillsbury Buttercream Frosting Mix may be substituted for milk chocolate frosting mix.

Spicy Butter Thins

1 cup (6-ounce package) butterscotch pieces
½ cup butter
¾ cup Pillsbury's Best All Purpose Flour
¼ cup sugar
1 teaspoon cinnamon
1 teaspoon instant coffee
½ teaspoon ginger
1 egg
½ cup chopped salted peanuts

OVEN 300°   36 BARS

In large saucepan melt ⅔ cup butterscotch pieces and butter over low heat, stirring constantly. Remove from heat. Add remaining ingredients except peanuts. Blend well.
Spread in well-greased 15x10x1-inch jelly roll pan. Sprinkle with ⅓ cup butterscotch pieces and peanuts. Bake at 300° for 20 to 25 minutes. Cool; cut into bars.

Golden Nut Drops

2 cups Pillsbury's Best All Purpose Flour
1½ teaspoons baking powder
½ teaspoon soda
¼ teaspoon salt
½ cup sugar
¼ cup firmly packed brown sugar
¾ cup shortening
1 egg
1 (4½-ounce) jar strained carrots
  baby food
1 teaspoon vanilla extract
1 cup chopped walnuts

OVEN 400°   54 TO 60 COOKIES

In large mixer bowl combine all ingredients except walnuts. Blend well with mixer. Stir in walnuts; mix thoroughly.

Drop by rounded teaspoon onto ungreased cookie sheets. Bake at 400° for 10 to 12 minutes. Frost with Vanilla Frosting while warm.

Vanilla Frosting

Prepare 1 package (small size) Pillsbury Buttercream Vanilla Frosting Mix as directed on package.
HIGH ALTITUDE ADJUSTMENT (5200 FEET)
Decrease baking powder to 1 teaspoon.

Heavenly Honey Bars

⅔ cup butter
½ cup honey
2 cups (7-ounce jar) marshmallow creme
2 eggs, slightly beaten
1 teaspoon vanilla extract
2 cups Pillsbury's Best All Purpose Flour
2 teaspoons baking powder
1 teaspoon salt
1 cup chopped nuts

OVEN 350°   36 BARS

In saucepan combine butter and honey over low heat, stirring constantly, until well blended. Cool slightly. Add marshmallow creme, eggs and vanilla extract; beat until well blended. Stir in remaining ingredients. Pour into greased 13x9-inch pan.

Bake at 350° for 25 to 30 minutes. Cool; cut into bars.

Spell-Binders

1½ cups Pillsbury's Best All Purpose Flour
1½ teaspoons baking powder
1 teaspoon soda
1 cup firmly packed brown sugar
1 cup butter, softened
1 egg
1 cup quick-cooking rolled oats
1 cup flaked coconut
1 cup salted Spanish peanuts
½ cup plus 2 tablespoons finely crushed
  corn flakes

OVEN 350°   48 TO 54 COOKIES

In large mixing bowl combine all ingredients except rolled oats, coconut, peanuts and corn flakes. Blend well with mixer. Stir in rolled oats, coconut, peanuts and ½ cup corn flake crumbs.

Drop by rounded teaspoon onto ungreased cookie sheets. Flatten slightly with bottom of glass dipped in remaining 2 tablespoons corn flakes.

Bake at 350° for 12 to 15 minutes. Drizzle with Icing.

Icing

Melt 2 tablespoons butter in 2-cup pyrex measuring cup. Add 1 cup confectioners' sugar, 1 tablespoon hot water and 1 teaspoon vanilla extract. Beat to consistency of a glaze.
HIGH ALTITUDE ADJUSTMENT (5200 FEET)
Oven temperature 375°. Decrease baking powder to 1 teaspoon.

Coco-nutty Brownies

1 cup (6-ounce package) semi-sweet
  chocolate pieces
½ cup butter
1 cup Pillsbury's Best All Purpose Flour
1 package (regular size) Pillsbury
  Coconut-Almond Frosting Mix
½ cup milk
1 egg
¼ teaspoon salt

In medium saucepan melt chocolate pieces and butter over low heat. Remove from heat. Add remaining ingredients. Beat until well blended.

Spread in greased 11x7 or 9x9-inch pan. Bake at 350° for 25 minutes. Cut into squares or bars. Cool.

Cookies To Travel

• Some cookies, like people, take to traveling better than others. A short trip to the beach or country in a picnic basket or an overseas package to your serviceman will make quite a difference in the kind of cookie and wrapping you choose.

Fragile cookies that crumble easily should not be packed for any lengthy journey. They are not really to be recommended even for short trips in the lunch box or picnic basket. Bars and drop cookies, especially those with fruit in to help keep them moist, and most molded cookies will pack well and arrive at their destination in the best condition. Brownies are especially good packables.

For the lunch box, try sandwiching two cookies together with a frosting between or use frostings that harden and will not stick to the wrapping. Frostings should be avoided on cookies being mailed a long distance because they may become dry and brittle and flake off the cookies.

Leave bar cookies in the pan they are baked in when packing the picnic basket. They will stay fresher and there is less danger of their breaking.

Packing Cookies for Mailing

Nothing is more welcome than cookies from home whether sent to a youngster at camp or school or a serviceman. Whatever the destination there are certain precautions to take in packing and shipping the cookies to make sure they are in good shape and edible on arrival. The length of the journey and destination also makes a difference in the type of packaging used.

Cardboard boxes of the heavy corrugated variety are convenient and satisfactory for most normal mail handling within the country. Metal containers such as empty 2 or 3 pound coffee cans are the most ideal for retaining moisture. They also give better protection in case the package is dropped. It is essential to use metal containers sealed air-tight as possible if the package is being sent to a tropical climate. With many servicemen overseas in hot humid countries, the food sent to them is likely to spoil unless sealed completely. It is also advisable to send several small packages under 5 pounds rather than one large package.

To cushion the cookies for their trip choose from excelsior, shredded paper, crumpled paper napkins, paper toweling or waxed paper. Unbuttered popcorn, a popular filler for domestic mailing, is not recommended for overseas mailing since it absorbs odors and moisture. But if it is used, a note should be included warning that it should not be eaten because it might cause illness.

Line the container with foil or plastic film

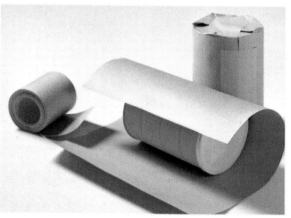

(not essential for metal cans). Wrap 4 to 6 of the same size cookies together in foil, plastic wrap or plastic bags and seal securely with freezer tape. Place the heaviest cookies in the bottom of the container and layer the wrapped cookies with the cushiony material mentioned above allowing space for a final layer of cushioning at the top of the container. Seal the top securely with freezer, plastic or adhesive tape.

Outer wrappings are equally important, especially for overseas mailing. Use plain heavy paper. The kind usually used in grocery store carry-out bags would be ideal.

See illustrations for wrapping both cardboard boxes and circular metal containers.

Print the mailing address as well as your return address on the package with permanent ink so it won't smear in case it is exposed to rain or snow. Covering the printing with clear plastic tape or colorless nail polish is another good idea. Be sure to mark the package "Perishable—Food" with the hope that it will receive more rapid and careful handling en route.

Fourth-class mail should be satisfactory for short domestic travel, however air mail is recommended for longer distances and definitely recommended for overseas shipment. Since mailing procedures vary with the location of military bases it is recommended that you contact your local Post Office for further information.

Almond Crunch Cookies

Nut-Dip
Orange
Drops

Mix'n
Match
Cookies

Fruitaroons

Almond Crunch Cookies

      3 cups Pillsbury's Best All Purpose Flour
      I teaspoon soda
      I teaspoon salt
      ½ teaspoon cream of tartar
      I cup sugar
      I cup firmly packed brown sugar
      ¾ cup shortening
      2 eggs
      I teaspoon vanilla extract
      I cup (5-ounce can) diced roasted almonds

OVEN 400°   60 TO 66 COOKIES

In large mixer bowl combine all ingredients except almonds. Blend well with mixer. Stir in almonds; mix thoroughly. If desired, chill for easier handling.

Shape dough into balls, using a rounded teaspoon for each. Place on ungreased cookie sheets.

Bake at 400° for 8 to 10 minutes. Cool.

Nut-Dip Orange Drops

      2 cups Pillsbury's Best All Purpose Flour
      I teaspoon soda
      I teaspoon salt
      ½ cup sugar
      ½ cup butter, softened
      ½ cup shortening
      ½ cup honey
      I egg
      I tablespoon prepared orange peel
      I½ cups chopped walnuts

OVEN 375°   48 TO 54 COOKIES

In large mixer bowl combine all ingredients except walnuts. Blend well with mixer. Stir in ½ cup walnuts; mix thoroughly. Chill at least I hour.

Drop by rounded teaspoon into remaining walnuts; roll to coat all sides. Place on greased cookie sheets.

Bake at 375° for 10 to 12 minutes. Cool I minute. Remove from cookie sheet.

Mix 'n Match Cookies

      2¼ cups Pillsbury's Best All Purpose Flour
      ½ teaspoon salt
      I cup sugar
      I cup shortening
      I egg
      I teaspoon vanilla extract
      I tablespoon milk
      ½ cup chopped walnuts
      ¼ cup molasses
      I cup flaked coconut

OVEN 350°   48 TO 54 COOKIES

In large mixer bowl combine flour, salt, sugar, shortening, egg and vanilla extract. Blend well with mixer. Place one-third of dough in small bowl. Add milk and walnuts. Stir molasses and coconut into remaining two-thirds of dough. Chill. Shape molasses dough into I-inch balls and place on ungreased cookie sheets. Shape walnut dough in ½-inch balls and place on top of each molasses ball. Flatten with bottom of glass, greased and dipped in sugar.

Bake at 350° for 15 to 18 minutes.

Fruitaroons

      I½ cups Pillsbury's Best All Purpose Flour
      ½ teaspoon baking powder
      ½ teaspoon soda
      ½ teaspoon salt
      I cup firmly packed brown sugar
      I egg
      2 tablespoons sour or sweet cream
      ⅓ cup shortening
      I½ cups flaked coconut
      I cup quick-cooking rolled oats
      I cup well drained fruit cocktail
      ½ cup chopped walnuts
      ¼ cup chopped maraschino cherries, drained

OVEN 375°   36 TO 42 COOKIES

In large mixer bowl combine all ingredients except coconut, rolled oats, fruit cocktail, walnuts and cherries. Blend well with mixer. Stir in remaining ingredients; mix thoroughly.

Drop by rounded teaspoon onto ungreased cookie sheets. Bake at 375° for 15 to 18 minutes. Cool.

Date Jewel Drops

    I cup finely cut dried apricots
I½ cups boiling water
2¼ cups Pillsbury's Best All Purpose Flour
    I teaspoon salt
    ½ teaspoon soda
    2 eggs
I¼ cups firmly packed brown sugar
    ¾ cup shortening
    I teaspoon vanilla extract
I¼ cups (8-ounce package) chopped dates

OVEN 375°   54 TO 60 COOKIES

Pour boiling water over apricots in small bowl. Let stand at least five minutes. Drain well.

In large mixer bowl combine remaining ingredients except dates. Blend well. Stir in apricots and dates. Mix thoroughly.

Drop by rounded teaspoon onto ungreased cookie sheets. Bake at 375° for 10 to 12 minutes. Cool.

Pick-Up Breaks

I¾ cups Pillsbury's Best All Purpose Flour
    ½ teaspoon baking powder
    ½ teaspoon salt
    ½ teaspoon soda
    ½ cup firmly packed brown sugar
    ½ cup butter, softened
    ½ cup peanut butter
    ½ cup maple flavored corn syrup
    ¼ cup frozen orange juice concentrate,
      thawed
    I egg
    I cup quick-cooking rolled oats
    I cup raisins

OVEN 350°   36 BARS

In large mixer bowl combine all ingredients except oats and raisins. Blend well with mixer. Blend in oats and raisins.

Spread in ungreased 15x10x1-inch jelly roll pan. Bake at 350° for 15 to 20 minutes. Cool. Cut into bars, squares or diamonds.

HIGH ALTITUDE ADJUSTMENT (5200 FEET)
Oven temperature 375°. Decrease baking powder to ¼ teaspoon.

Apricot Chews

½ cup finely cut dried apricots
½ cup raisins
⅓ cup water
1 cup Pillsbury's Best All Purpose Flour
1 teaspoon baking powder
¼ teaspoon soda
1 cup sugar
2 eggs
1 tablespoon lemon juice
½ cup drained crushed pineapple
½ cup chopped walnuts
Confectioners' sugar

OVEN 350°   24 BARS

In large saucepan combine apricots, raisins and water. Cook over low heat, stirring occasionally, until water is absorbed. Cool slightly. Add remaining ingredients except confectioners' sugar. Blend well. Spread in greased 9-inch square pan.

Bake at 350° for 35 to 40 minutes. While warm, cut in bars. Sprinkle with confectioners' sugar.
HIGH ALTITUDE ADJUSTMENT (5200 FEET)
Oven temperature 375°.

Jumble Brownies

1¼ cups Pillsbury's Best All Purpose Flour
1¼ cups sugar
⅓ cup cocoa
½ teaspoon baking powder
½ teaspoon salt
⅔ cup shortening
2 eggs
1 tablespoon light corn syrup
1 teaspoon vanilla extract
1 (4¾ ounce) jar strained prune baby food
½ cup chopped walnuts
½ cup flaked coconut

OVEN 350°   36 BARS

In large mixer bowl combine all ingredients except walnuts and coconut. Blend well with mixer. Stir in remaining ingredients. Mix thoroughly. Spread in greased 13x9-inch pan.

Bake at 350° for 30 to 35 minutes. Cut into bars while warm. Cool.

Lemon Lassies

Lemon Filling:
> 2 eggs
> ½ cup sugar
> I tablespoon prepared lemon peel
> ¼ cup lemon juice
> I tablespoon butter
> ⅛ teaspoon salt
> I cup flaked coconut

Cookie dough:
> 2¼ cups Pillsbury's Best All Purpose Flour
> I teaspoon cinnamon
> ½ teaspoon soda
> ¼ teaspoon salt
> I cup sugar
> ½ cup butter, softened
> ¼ cup molasses
> I egg

In a small saucepan combine all Filling ingredients except coconut. Cook over low heat, stirring constantly, until thick. Remove from heat; add coconut. Cool.

In large mixer bowl combine all ingredients for cookie dough. Blend well with mixer. Divide dough into 4 parts.

Shape each into a 15-inch roll on an ungreased cookie sheet. Flatten each roll to a 2½-inch strip.

Spread ¼ amount of Filling down center of each strip. Roll dough to center covering filling.

Bake at 350° for 12 to 15 minutes. Cut while warm into I-inch pieces.

Butter-Nut Bars

Crust:
> I cup Pillsbury's Best All Purpose Flour
> ¼ teaspoon salt
> ½ cup firmly packed brown sugar
> ⅓ cup butter, softened

Topping:
> ¼ teaspoon salt
> I tablespoon butter
> I cup (6-ounce package) butterscotch pieces
> ¼ cup light corn syrup
> I tablespoon water
> ½ cup chopped walnuts

In small mixer bowl combine all ingredients for Crust. Blend with mixer until particles are fine. Press in ungreased 8-inch square pan. Bake at 375° for 10 minutes.

In medium saucepan combine all ingredients for Topping except walnuts. Cook over low heat until butterscotch pieces are melted. Stir in walnuts. Spread evenly over partially baked crumb crust.

Bake at 375° for 8 to 10 minutes. Cool; cut into small bars.

Southern Pecan Bars

Crumb Crust:
> 1⅓ cups Pillsbury's Best All Purpose Flour
> ½ cup firmly packed brown sugar
> ½ teaspoon baking powder
> ⅓ cup butter, softened
> ¼ cup chopped pecans

Topping:
> ¾ cup dark corn syrup
> ¼ cup firmly packed brown sugar
> 3 tablespoons Pillsbury's Best All Purpose Flour
> ½ teaspoon salt
> 2 eggs
> I teaspoon vanilla extract
> ¾ cup chopped pecans

In large mixer bowl combine all ingredients for crumb crust except pecans. Blend with mixer until particles are fine. Stir in pecans. Press in greased 13x9-inch pan.

In same mixer bowl combine all ingredients for topping except pecans. Blend well. Pour over crumb crust. Sprinkle with pecans.

Bake at 350° for 25 to 30 minutes. Cool; cut into bars.

Pineapple Brownies

1½ cups Pillsbury's Best All Purpose Flour
1½ cups sugar
   1 teaspoon baking powder
   ½ teaspoon salt
   ½ teaspoon cinnamon
   ¾ cup butter, softened
   3 eggs
   1 teaspoon vanilla extract
   1 cup well-drained crushed pineapple
   2 (1-ounce) envelopes premelted
      unsweetened chocolate
   ½ cup chopped walnuts

OVEN 375°   30 BARS

In large mixer bowl combine all ingredients except pineapple, chocolate and walnuts. Blend well with mixer.

Place half of dough in small bowl. Add pineapple; mix well. To remaining dough, add chocolate and walnuts; mix well.

Spread chocolate mixture in bottom of greased 13x9-inch pan. Spread pineapple mixture over chocolate layer. Using a knife, marbelize. Bake at 375° for 35 to 40 minutes. Cool; cut into bars.

Candy Surprises

   2 cups Pillsbury's Best All Purpose Flour
   1½ teaspoons baking powder
   ¼ teaspoon salt
   1½ cups firmly packed brown sugar
   ½ cup butter, softened
   2 eggs
   1 teaspoon vanilla extract
   ½ cup creamy peanut butter
   8 (⅞-ounce) milk chocolate candy bars
      Confectioners' sugar

OVEN 350°   36 BARS

In large mixer bowl combine all ingredients except peanut butter, candy and confectioners' sugar. Blend well.

Spread half of dough in an ungreased 11x7-inch pan. Place candy bars over dough. Spoon peanut butter over candy; spread carefully to cover. Spread remaining dough over peanut butter.

Bake at 350° for 30 to 35 minutes. Cool thoroughly. Sprinkle with confectioners' sugar. Cut into bars.

Butterscotch Oaties

   1 cup Pillsbury's Best All Purpose Flour
   1½ cups sugar
   ½ teaspoon salt
   ¾ cup milk
   ¼ cup butter
   1 cup (6-ounce package) butterscotch
      pieces
   2½ cups quick-cooking rolled oats
   1 cup flaked coconut
   1 cup chopped walnuts
   1 teaspoon vanilla extract

OVEN 325°   36 COOKIES

In large saucepan combine flour, sugar, salt, milk and butter. Bring to a boil, over low heat, stirring occasionally. Boil 3 minutes, stirring constantly. Remove from heat.

Stir in butterscotch pieces and remaining ingredients; mix well.

Drop by tablespoon onto lightly greased cookie sheets. Bake at 325° for 12 to 15 minutes. Cool slightly; remove from sheets.

Lemon Lassies

Pineapple Brownies

Candy Surprises

Butter-Nut Bars

Butterscotch Oaties

Southern Pecan Bars

Steady Daters

Chewy Cranberry Gingers

Cherry Fancy

Butterscotch Fudge Bars

Butteroons

Macadamia Nut Cookies

Chewy Cranberry Gingers

2⅓ cups Pillsbury's Best All Purpose Flour
2 teaspoons soda
½ teaspoon salt
1 teaspoon cinnamon
½ teaspoon ginger
1 cup sugar
¾ cup shortening
1 egg
¼ cup molasses
½ cup whole cranberry sauce
  (cooked or canned)

OVEN 375°   60 TO 66 COOKIES

In large mixer bowl combine all ingredients except cranberries. Blend well. Stir in cranberries; mix thoroughly. Chill dough at least 1 hour.

Shape into balls using a rounded teaspoon. Coat with additional sugar. Place on ungreased cookie sheets.

Bake at 375° for 12 to 15 minutes. Remove from cookie sheet immediately.
HIGH ALTITUDE ADJUSTMENT (5200 FEET)
Decrease soda to 1 teaspoon, sugar to ¾ cup and shortening to ½ cup.

Butterscotch Fudge Bars

½ cup butter
1 (1-ounce) envelope premelted
  unsweetened chocolate
1½ cups Pillsbury's Best All Purpose Flour
½ teaspoon soda
2 cups firmly packed brown sugar
2 eggs
1 teaspoon vanilla extract
¾ cup chopped walnuts
  Confectioners' sugar

OVEN 350°   36 BARS

In large saucepan melt butter and chocolate over low heat. Remove from heat. Add remaining ingredients except confectioners' sugar. Blend well.

Spread in greased 13x9-inch pan. Bake at 350° for 25 to 30 minutes.

Cool; sprinkle with confectioners' sugar. Cut into bars.

Steady Daters

Cookie dough:
2½ cups Pillsbury's Best All Purpose Flour
1 teaspoon salt
1 cup butter, softened
6 to 8 tablespoons cold water
  Sugar to sprinkle

Date-Peanut Butter Filling:
1 (12-ounce) can date cake and pastry
  filling
2 tablespoons peanut butter

OVEN 400°   30 TO 36 SANDWICH COOKIES

In large mixer bowl combine flour, salt and butter. Blend with mixer until particles are fine. Sprinkle cold water over mixture while tossing and stirring lightly with a fork until dough is just moist enough to hold together.

Roll out half of dough on floured surface to ⅛-inch thickness. Cut with 2-inch round cutter. Place on ungreased cookie sheets.

Combine Filling ingredients; blend well. Place a teaspoon of Date-Peanut Butter Filling in center of each cookie.

Roll out remaining dough, cut with cutter, place rounds over top of filling and press edges together to seal. Sprinkle with sugar.

Bake at 400° for 12 to 15 minutes. Cool.

Cherry Fancy

¾ cup granulated brown sugar
3 tablespoons butter, softened
½ cup Pillsbury's Best All Purpose Flour
1½ teaspoons pumpkin pie spice
¼ teaspoon soda
1 egg
1 cup chopped walnuts
⅓ cup sugar
¼ cup chopped maraschino cherries
2 tablespoons grated orange peel

OVEN 350°   24 BARS

In large mixer bowl combine brown sugar, butter, flour, pumpkin pie spice, soda and egg. Blend well with mixer. Stir in walnuts. Spread in greased 9-inch square pan.

Combine sugar, cherries and orange peel; mix well. Sprinkle over batter. Bake at 350° for 20 to 25 minutes. Cool; cut into bars.
HIGH ALTITUDE ADJUSTMENT (5200 FEET)
Oven temperature 375°. Increase flour to ¾ cup.

Butteroons

1 egg, separated
1 cup Pillsbury's Best All Purpose Flour
¼ teaspoon salt
⅓ cup sugar
½ cup butter, softened
2 teaspoons prepared lemon peel
½ cup finely chopped candied pineapple
1 cup flaked coconut

OVEN 325°   30 TO 36 COOKIES

In large mixer bowl combine egg yolk and remaining ingredients except coconut. Blend well with mixer. Chill dough for easier handling.

Shape in balls, using a teaspoon for each. Dip top in slightly beaten egg white, then in coconut. Place on ungreased cookie sheets.

Bake at 325° for 20 to 25 minutes until light golden brown.

Macadamia Nut Cookies

¾ cup butter, softened
½ cup firmly packed brown sugar
2 tablespoons milk
1½ teaspoons cinnamon
2 cups Pillsbury's Best All Purpose Flour
1 tablespoon baking powder
¾ teaspoon salt
¾ cup coarsely chopped macadamia nuts
½ cup finely chopped candied pineapple
Sugar

OVEN 375°   48 TO 54 COOKIES

In large mixer bowl, combine all ingredients except nuts and pineapple. Blend well with mixer to form a stiff dough. Stir in nuts and pineapple. Drop by teaspoon onto ungreased cookie sheets. Flatten with bottom of glass which has been dipped in sugar. Bake at 375° for 7 to 10 minutes.

Oatmeal Take-Alongs

By Cracky Bars

Minnesota Harvest Bars

Oatmeal Take-Alongs

    3 cups Pillsbury's Best All Purpose Flour
    2 cups sugar
    2 teaspoons soda
 1½ teaspoons salt
    1 cup shortening
    ½ cup molasses
    2 eggs
 1½ teaspoons vanilla extract
    2 cups quick-cooking rolled oats
    1 cup flaked coconut

OVEN 375°   72 TO 78 COOKIES

In large mixer bowl combine all ingredients except rolled oats and coconut. Blend well with mixer. Stir in remaining ingredients; mix thoroughly.

Drop by rounded teaspoon onto greased cookie sheets. Bake at 375° for 10 to 12 minutes. If desired, frost while warm with Chocolate Frosting.

Chocolate Frosting

Combine ⅓ cup light cream and ½ cup sugar in small saucepan. Bring to a full boil; remove from heat. Stir in 1 cup (6-ounce package) semi-sweet chocolate pieces.

Minnesota Harvest Bars

    ¼ cup shortening
    ¾ cup Pillsbury's Best All Purpose Flour
    ½ teaspoon baking powder
    ½ teaspoon salt
    ¼ teaspoon soda
    ½ teaspoon cinnamon
    ½ teaspoon nutmeg
    ½ teaspoon ginger
    ½ teaspoon vanilla extract
    2 eggs
    1 cup firmly packed brown sugar
    ⅔ cup canned pumpkin
    ½ cup chopped dates
    ½ cup chopped walnuts
      Confectioners' sugar

OVEN 350°   32 BARS

In large saucepan melt shortening over low heat. Remove from heat. Add remaining ingredients except confectioners' sugar. Blend well. Pour into greased 13x9-inch pan.

Bake at 350° for 25 to 30 minutes. Cool; cut into bars. Sprinkle with confectioners' sugar.

By Cracky Bars

 1¾ cups Pillsbury's Best All Purpose Flour
    ½ teaspoon salt
    ¼ teaspoon soda
    ¾ cup butter, softened
    1 cup sugar
    ⅓ cup milk
    2 eggs
    1 teaspoon vanilla extract
    1 (1-ounce) envelope premelted
      unsweetened chocolate
    ¾ cup chopped walnuts
   15 single graham crackers
    1 cup (6-ounce package) semi-sweet
      chocolate pieces

OVEN 375°   36 BARS

In large mixer bowl combine all ingredients except chocolate, walnuts, crackers and chocolate pieces. Blend well.

To half of dough, in another bowl, add envelope of chocolate and nuts. Spread in greased 13x9-inch pan. Arrange crackers over dough. Add chocolate pieces to remaining dough. Drop by tablespoon over crackers and spread carefully to cover.

Bake at 375° for 25 to 30 minutes. Cool; cut into bars.

Chocolate Cookie Rolls

Cookie dough:
>   2 cups Pillsbury's Best All Purpose Flour
> ½ teaspoon baking powder
> ¾ cup butter, softened
>   2 teaspoons vanilla extract
>   1 egg
> ¼ cup finely grated coconut
>   1 package (small size) Pillsbury
>   Buttercream Fudge Frosting Mix

Filling:
>   2 tablespoons butter, softened
>   1 egg
> ½ cup flaked coconut
> ⅓ cup Pillsbury's Best Flour

OVEN 350°   60 COOKIES

In large mixer bowl combine flour, baking powder, butter, vanilla extract, egg, coconut and 1 cup firmly packed dry frosting mix. Reserve remaining dry frosting mix for Filling. Blend well with mixer.

In mixer bowl combine Filling ingredients with reserved dry frosting mix. Beat until well blended with mixer.

Divide dough into four portions. With well-floured hands, shape each portion into a strip 2 inches wide and about 15 inches long on ungreased cookie sheets. Make a depression 1 inch wide and ¾ inch deep down center of each strip; spread with Filling. Bake at 350° for 15 to 20 minutes. While warm, cut into 1-inch slices. Cool.

Fruit Punch Bars

>   2 eggs
> 1½ cups sugar
>   1 (1 pound 1-ounce) can fruit cocktail,
>   undrained
> 2¼ cups Pillsbury's Best All Purpose Flour
> 1½ teaspoons soda
> ½ teaspoon salt
>   1 teaspoon vanilla extract
> 1⅓ cups flaked coconut
> ½ cup chopped pecans

OVEN 350°   36 TO 40 BARS

In large mixer bowl beat eggs and sugar until light and fluffy. Add remaining ingredients except coconut and pecans. Blend well with mixer.

Choco-Date Squares

Crust:
> ½ cup butter
> ½ cup semi-sweet chocolate pieces
> 1⅓ cups Pillsbury's Best All Purpose Flour
> ¼ cup sugar

Filling:
> ¼ cup butter, softened
> ¾ cup confectioners' sugar
> ½ teaspoon baking powder
>   2 eggs
>   2 tablespoons water
> ¾ cup creamy peanut butter
> ¾ cup chopped dates
> ¾ cup chopped walnuts

OVEN 350°   48 SQUARES

Melt ½ cup butter with ½ cup chocolate pieces in saucepan over low heat, stirring constantly. Remove from heat. Add flour and sugar. Press in ungreased 13x9-inch pan.

In large mixer bowl combine ¼ cup butter, confectioners' sugar, baking powder, eggs, water and peanut butter. Blend well. Stir in dates and walnuts; mix thoroughly. Spread over chocolate crust.

Bake at 350° for 30 to 35 minutes. Cool. Spread with Frosting. If desired, sprinkle with chopped walnuts.

Frosting

Melt ½ cup semi-sweet chocolate pieces and 1 tablespoon shortening in saucepan.

Spread in greased and floured 15x10x1-inch jelly roll pan. Sprinkle with coconut and pecans. Bake at 350° for 25 to 30 minutes or until golden brown. While hot, drizzle with Glaze. Cool; cut into bars.

Glaze ¾ cup sugar
> ½ cup butter
> ¼ cup evaporated milk
> ½ teaspoon vanilla extract
> ½ cup chopped pecans

In small saucepan combine all ingredients except pecans. Bring to a boil; boil 2 minutes, stirring constantly. Remove from heat; stir in pecans. Cool.

HIGH ALTITUDE ADJUSTMENT (5200 FEET)
Oven temperature 375°. Decrease sugar to 1¼ cups and soda to 1¼ teaspoons.

Redi-Frosted Raisin Bars

Crust:
- 1 cup sugar
- 1 cup raisins
- 1 cup water
- ½ cup butter
- 1 teaspoon cinnamon
- ½ teaspoon cloves
- ¼ teaspoon nutmeg
- ¼ teaspoon salt
- 2 cups Pillsbury's Best All Purpose Flour
- 1 teaspoon soda
- ½ teaspoon baking powder
- 1 teaspoon vanilla extract

Topping:
- 1 cup firmly packed brown sugar
- ½ cup chopped walnuts
- ¼ cup Pillsbury's Best All Purpose Flour
- 2 tablespoons butter, melted
- 1 tablespoon cinnamon

OVEN 350°   36 BARS

In 2-quart saucepan, combine all ingredients except flour, soda, baking powder and vanilla extract. Bring to a boil; boil gently 3 minutes. Cool. Add remaining ingredients; blend well. Spread batter evenly in greased 15x10x1-inch jelly roll pan.

Combine all ingredients for topping and mix well. Sprinkle evenly over batter; press down lightly.

Bake at 350° for 20 to 25 minutes. Cool; cut into bars.

HIGH ALTITUDE ADJUSTMENT (5200 FEET)
Oven temperature 375°. Decrease soda to ½ teaspoon.

Cashew Caramel Yummies

Cookie dough:
- ¾ cup Pillsbury's Best All Purpose Flour
- ½ teaspoon baking powder
- ¼ teaspoon salt
- ½ cup sugar
- ½ cup firmly packed brown sugar
- 2 eggs
- ½ cup chopped salted cashews

Cashew Topping:
- 2 tablespoons butter
- ¼ cup firmly packed brown sugar
- 1½ tablespoons cream
- ½ cup chopped salted cashews

Pebble Top Chocolate Bars

Crust:
- 1½ cups flaked coconut
- 2 tablespoons butter, melted
- 2 tablespoons sugar
- ¼ cup graham cracker crumbs

Topping:
- ½ cup butter, softened
- ½ cup sugar
- ¼ cup firmly packed brown sugar
- 1 egg
- 1 teaspoon vanilla extract
- 2 tablespoons milk
- 1 cup Pillsbury's Best All Purpose Flour
- ½ teaspoon soda
- ½ teaspoon salt
- 1 cup (6-ounce package) semi-sweet chocolate pieces
- ½ cup chopped pecans
- 1 cup (8-ounce package) candied fruits and peels

OVEN 350°   18 BARS

In bottom of 9-inch square pan, combine coconut, melted butter, 2 tablespoons sugar and graham cracker crumbs. Mix well; spread evenly in bottom of pan. Pat down gently.

In large mixer bowl, combine ingredients for topping except chocolate pieces, pecans and fruit. Blend well with mixer. Stir in chocolate pieces and pecans. Spread over crust. Top with fruit.

Bake at 350° for 35 to 40 minutes. Cool; cut into bars.

OVEN 350°   36 BARS

In large mixer bowl combine all ingredients for cookie dough except cashews. Blend well with mixer. Stir in cashews. Spread in greased 9-inch square pan. Bake at 350° for 20 to 25 minutes.

Spread immediately with Cashew Topping, covering top completely. Broil until lightly browned, 1 to 3 minutes, watching carefully. While warm, cut into bars.

Cashew Topping: Melt butter in medium saucepan. Remove from heat. Add remaining ingredients.

Peanut Butter Fingers

> 1 cup Pillsbury's Best All Purpose Flour
> ½ cup sugar
> ½ cup firmly packed brown sugar
> ½ teaspoon soda
> ¼ teaspoon salt
> ½ cup butter, softened
> ⅓ cup creamy peanut butter
> 1 egg
> ½ teaspoon vanilla extract
> 1 cup quick-cooking rolled oats
> 1 cup (6-ounce package) semi-sweet
> chocolate pieces

OVEN 350°   48 BARS

In large mixer bowl combine all ingredients except chocolate pieces. Blend with mixer until particles are coarse crumbs. Press in greased 13x9-inch pan.

Bake at 350° for 20 to 25 minutes. Sprinkle immediately with chocolate pieces. Let stand 5 minutes. Spread evenly. Drizzle with Peanut Butter mixture. Cool; cut into bars.

Peanut Butter Drizzle

Combine ½ cup sifted confectioners' sugar, ¼ cup creamy peanut butter and 2 to 4 tablespoons milk; mix well.

Bars O' Maple

> ¾ cup Pillsbury's Best All Purpose Flour
> ½ teaspoon salt
> ¼ teaspoon soda
> ⅓ cup butter, softened
> ⅓ cup confectioners' sugar
> ⅓ cup maple syrup
> ½ teaspoon maple flavoring
> 1 egg
> 1 cup chopped walnuts

OVEN 375°   18 BARS

In large mixer bowl combine all ingredients for bars except walnuts. Blend well with mixer. Stir in walnuts.

Spread in greased 8-inch square pan. Bake at 375° for 15 to 18 minutes. Frost while warm. Cool. Cut in bars.

Maple Frosting

Prepare 1 package (small size) Pillsbury Buttercream Vanilla Frosting Mix as directed on package adding ⅛ to ¼ teaspoon maple flavoring to water.

Fresh Orange Chewies

> 2 medium oranges
> 1½ cups firmly packed brown sugar
> 2 eggs
> 1⅓ cups Pillsbury's Best All Purpose Flour
> ¾ teaspoon baking powder
> ½ teaspoon salt
> ⅔ cup chopped walnuts

OVEN 350°   24 TO 30 BARS

Grate oranges to obtain 1 tablespoon orange rind; set aside. Peel and section oranges; chop and set aside.

In large mixer bowl beat sugar and eggs at high speed of mixer for 3 minutes. Fold in flour, baking powder, salt, walnuts and oranges. Spread batter in greased and floured 13x9-inch pan.

Bake at 350° for 30 to 35 minutes until golden brown. Cool. Frost and cut into bars.

Frosting

In small mixer bowl combine 1 package (small size) Pillsbury Buttercream Vanilla Frosting Mix, 2 tablespoons butter, softened, 2 tablespoons lukewarm water and orange rind. Blend well with mixer.

Penuche Chews

> 1½ cups firmly packed brown sugar
> ¾ cup butter
> ½ cup milk
> 2 cups Pillsbury's Best All Purpose Flour
> 1 teaspoon salt
> ½ teaspoon soda
> 1 cup confectioners' sugar
> 1 teaspoon vanilla extract
> 1 cup chopped walnuts

OVEN 375°   60 BARS

In large saucepan combine brown sugar, butter and milk. Bring to a boil over medium heat, stirring constantly; boil 1 minute. Remove from heat. Add remaining ingredients except walnuts. Blend well. Stir in walnuts.

Spread in well-greased 15x10x1-inch jelly roll pan. Bake at 375° for 20 to 25 minutes. (Do not overbake.) Frost while warm. Cool; cut into bars.

Brown Sugar Frosting

Prepare 1 package (regular size) Pillsbury Buttercream Brown Sugar Frosting Mix as directed on package following *cooked* version.

HIGH ALTITUDE ADJUSTMENT (5200 FEET)
Decrease brown sugar to 1¼ cups and butter to ½ cup.

Choco-Date Squares

Fruit Punch Bars

Redi-Frosted
Raisin Bars

Pebble Top
Chocolate Bars

Chocolate Cookie Rolls

Peanut Butter Fingers

Fresh
Orange
Chewies

Bars
O'Maple

Penuche Chews

Cashew Caramel Yummies

Party Cookies

• Plain or fancy cookies are ideal party fare. While the fancier cookies may be a little more time consuming to prepare consider how much they will contribute to the appearance of your party table. Used as a centerpiece in a cornucopia or handsome tiered tray they can also be a conversation piece.

A reception or tea table is even more festive with an attractive assortment of dainty molded or pressed cookies frosted and decorated with a variety of toppings. If you are planning your table decorations around a color scheme, for example pink and white for a bridal shower, you might use pink and white frostings on the cookies and decorate them with bits of candied cherry and silver balls to carry out the theme. Cake and cookie decorator in the handy push button can makes it easy to add frosting rose buds or other decorations to your party cookies.

For children's parties, make place cards with large round or rectangular refrigerator cookies colorfully decorated with the push button cookie decorator. Write each youngster's name in frosting on the cookies. Make a slit in a large gum drop to hold the cookie and stand one at each place.

Decorated cut-out animal cookies and clowns can set the spirit for a circus party. Stand them up by inserting in large gum drops. Gingerbread men in a variety of poses will entertain as well as satisfy the appetites of the younger set.

Teen-agers prefer less sophisticated fare for their parties. Brownies rate number one in popularity followed by dream bars and drop cookies. Anything chocolate wins the boys' vote followed by peanut butter. Whether after the game open house, slumber party or graduation parties the most important thing is to have plenty on hand.

Almond Party Press Cookies

Praline Cookies

Snowball Cookies

Almond Coconut Twinkles

Jamerangs

Lemon Mardi Gras Squares

Meringue topped Almondettes

Almond Party Press Cookies

2¼ cups Pillsbury's Best All Purpose Flour
½ teaspoon cardamom
¼ teaspoon salt
¾ cup sugar
1 cup butter, softened
1 egg
2 tablespoons milk
½ cup almond paste

OVEN 350°   54 TO 60 COOKIES

In large mixer bowl combine all ingredients. Blend well with mixer.

Press through cookie press onto ungreased cookie sheets, using any plate to make desired shapes.

Bake at 350° for 10 to 12 minutes.

Snowball Cookies

1 cup Pillsbury's Best All Purpose Flour
¼ teaspoon salt
⅓ cup sugar
½ cup butter, softened
1 egg
1 teaspoon vanilla extract
2 cups flaked coconut

OVEN 350°   36 COOKIES

In large mixer bowl combine all ingredients except coconut. Blend well with mixer. Chill dough while toasting coconut.

Toast coconut by spreading on cookie sheet and placing in 350° oven for 5 to 8 minutes, stirring occasionally.

Drop dough by rounded teaspoon onto ungreased cookie sheets. Bake at 350° for 15 to 18 minutes. Cool.

Dip cookie in Frosting then in toasted coconut. Let stand until Frosting is set.

Fluffy White Frosting

Prepare 1 package (regular size) Pillsbury Fluffy White Frosting Mix as directed on package.

Lemon Mardi Gras Squares

    3 eggs, separated
    1 cup confectioners' sugar
1½ cups Pillsbury's Best All Purpose Flour
    1 cup sugar
    ½ teaspoon salt
    ¼ teaspoon baking powder
    ½ cup butter, softened
    ⅓ cup lemon juice
    2 tablespoons prepared lemon peel
    ¾ cup chopped pecans

OVEN 400°   36 BARS

In small mixer bowl beat egg whites until soft mounds form. Gradually add confectioners' sugar and continue beating until stiff peaks form. Set aside.

In large mixer bowl combine egg yolks and remaining ingredients except pecans. Blend well. Stir in ½ cup pecans. Fold in beaten egg whites gently but thoroughly.

Spread in greased and lightly floured 13x9-inch pan. Bake at 400° for 25 to 30 minutes. Frost while warm. Sprinkle with ¼ cup pecans. Cut into bars.

Vanilla Frosting

Prepare 1 package (small size) Pillsbury Butter-cream Vanilla Frosting Mix as directed on package.

Jamerangs

Cookie dough:
    1¼ cups Pillsbury's Best All Purpose Flour
    1 teaspoon baking powder
    ½ cup sugar
    ⅓ cup butter, softened
    1 egg yolk
    1 tablespoon milk
    ½ teaspoon vanilla extract

Topping:
    ⅓ cup apricot preserves
    1 teaspoon lemon juice

Meringue:
    1 egg white
    5 tablespoons sugar
    ½ teaspoon cinnamon
    ⅓ cup chopped walnuts

OVEN 350°   30 TO 36 COOKIES

In large mixer bowl combine all ingredients except apricot preserves and lemon juice. Blend well with mixer.

Shape into balls using a teaspoon for each. Place on greased cookie sheets and flatten to ¼-inch thickness.

Combine preserves and lemon juice. Place ¼ teaspoon on top of each cookie.

Prepare meringue by beating egg white in small mixer bowl until soft mounds form. Gradually add sugar and continue beating until stiff peaks form. Fold in cinnamon and walnuts. Place a teaspoon of meringue on each cookie, covering jam completely.

Bake at 350° for 12 to 15 minutes until meringue is light brown.

Meringue-topped Almondettes

Cookie dough:
    2 egg yolks
    2 cups Pillsbury's Best All Purpose Flour
    ¾ teaspoon salt
    ½ teaspoon soda
    ⅔ cup sugar
    ⅓ cup firmly packed brown sugar
    ½ cup shortening
    ¼ cup butter, softened
    2 tablespoons cream or milk
    1 teaspoon almond extract
    ½ cup slivered almonds
    ½ cup flaked coconut

Almond Meringue:
    2 egg whites
    ¼ teaspoon salt
    ⅓ cup sugar
    ½ teaspoon almond extract
    1 cup slivered almonds
    1 cup flaked coconut

OVEN 375°   50 TO 56 COOKIES

In large mixer bowl combine all cookie dough ingredients except almonds and coconut. Blend well with mixer. Stir in almonds and coconut; mix thoroughly.

Shape into balls using a rounded teaspoon for each. Place on ungreased cookie sheets. Flatten with bottom of a glass dipped in sugar.

Prepare Almond Meringue by beating egg whites and salt in small mixer bowl until soft mounds form. Gradually add sugar and continue beating until stiff peaks form. Fold in remaining ingredients. Place a rounded teaspoon on top of each cookie.

Bake at 375° for 12 to 15 minutes.

Almond-Coconut Twinkles

    1¼ cups Pillsbury's Best All Purpose Flour
    1 teaspoon baking powder
    ¼ teaspoon salt
    ⅔ cup sugar
    ½ cup shortening
    2 egg whites
    ½ teaspoon vanilla extract
    ½ teaspoon almond extract
    1 cup flaked coconut

OVEN 375°   30 TO 36 COOKIES

In large mixer bowl combine all ingredients except coconut. Blend well with mixer. Stir in coconut; mix thoroughly.

Drop by rounded teaspoon onto greased cookie sheets. Bake at 375° for 10 to 12 minutes. Cool. If desired, frost with Chocolate Almond Frosting.

Chocolate Almond Frosting

Prepare 1 package (small size) Pillsbury Buttercream Fudge Frosting Mix as directed on package adding ½ teaspoon almond extract to water.

Praline Cookies

    1½ cups Pillsbury's Best All Purpose Flour
    1½ teaspoons baking powder
    ½ teaspoon salt
    1½ cups firmly packed brown sugar
    ⅔ cup shortening
    1 egg
    1 teaspoon vanilla extract
    ½ cup coarsely chopped pecans

OVEN 350°   48 TO 54 COOKIES

In large mixer bowl combine all ingredients except pecans. Blend well. Drop by teaspoon onto greased cookie sheets.

Bake at 350° for 10 to 12 minutes. Cool. Top each cookie with ½ teaspoon pecans. Drizzle with Brown Sugar Frosting.

Brown Sugar Frosting

Prepare 1 package (regular size) Pillsbury Buttercream Brown Sugar Frosting Mix following recipe for *cooked* version.

71

Macaroon Polka Dots

Crust:
- *1 cup Pillsbury's Best All Purpose Flour*
- *½ cup firmly packed brown sugar*
- *¼ teaspoon soda*
- *¼ teaspoon salt*
- *⅓ cup butter, softened*
- *1 teaspoon vanilla extract*
- *2 egg yolks*

Macaroon Topping:
- *2 egg whites*
- *1 tablespoon sugar*
- *¾ cup sweetened condensed milk*
- *½ cup semi-sweet chocolate pieces*
- *2 cups (7-ounce package) finely grated coconut*

OVEN 325°   36 BARS

In small mixer bowl combine all ingredients for crust. Blend with mixer until particles are fine. Press in greased 11x7-inch pan.

Bake at 325° for 12 to 15 minutes. Do not brown.

Prepare Macaroon Topping by beating egg whites in large mixer bowl until soft mounds form. Add sugar; continue beating until stiff peaks form. Fold in remaining ingredients. Spread evenly over crust.

Bake at 325° for 25 to 30 minutes. Cool; cut into bars.

Split Levels

Chocolate Filling:
   1 cup (6-ounce package) semi-sweet
      chocolate pieces
   1 (3-ounce) package cream cheese
   ⅓ cup evaporated milk
   ½ cup chopped walnuts
   2 tablespoons sesame seed
   ¼ teaspoon almond extract

Crumb crust:
   1½ cups Pillsbury's Best All Purpose Flour
   ½ teaspoon baking powder
   ¼ teaspoon salt
   ¾ cup sugar
   ½ cup butter, softened
      1 egg
   ¼ teaspoon almond extract

OVEN 375°   24 BARS

In saucepan combine chocolate pieces, cream cheese and milk. Melt over low heat, stirring constantly. Remove from heat. Stir in remaining filling ingredients. Blend well. Set aside.

In large mixer bowl combine all crust ingredients. Blend well with mixer until particles are fine.

Press half of crumb crust mixture in greased 11x7-inch pan. Spread with filling. Sprinkle rest of crumbs over filling.

Bake at 375° for 20 to 25 minutes. Cool.

Honey Bunches

    3 cups quick-cooking rolled oats
    2 cups flaked coconut
    1 cup Pillsbury's Best All Purpose Flour
  1½ cups firmly packed brown sugar
    1 cup butter
    ⅓ cup honey

OVEN 350°   50 COOKIES

In large mixing bowl combine oats, coconut and flour. In heavy saucepan combine remaining ingredients and bring to a boil. Pour over dry ingredients; blend well.

Drop dough by teaspoons into greased muffin cups or foil baking cups on cookie sheet. Bake at 350° for 12 to 15 minutes or until well browned. Cool in pans.

Tip: If desired, 1 cup chopped walnuts and 1 cup flaked coconut may be substituted for the 2 cups coconut.

Lemon-Cheese Pillows

Crust:

    1 cup butter, softened
    2 (3-ounce) packages cream cheese,
      softened
    ¼ cup confectioners' sugar
    2¼ cups Pillsbury's Best All Purpose Flour
    1 teaspoon grated lemon peel
    1 teaspoon lemon juice

Filling:

    3 cups (1-pound carton) dry cottage cheese
    2 eggs
    1 cup sugar
    ½ cup Pillsbury's Best All Purpose Flour
    ¼ cup lemon juice
    1 tablespoon grated lemon peel

OVEN 350°   36 COOKIES

In large mixer bowl, combine all ingredients for crust. Blend with mixer until a dough forms. Cover; chill 30 minutes.

In large saucepan, combine filling ingredients; blend well. Cook over medium heat, stirring constantly, until thick.

Divide dough into 4 parts; roll each on floured surface to a 9-inch square. Cut into 3-inch squares. Place 1 tablespoon filling in center of each square. Fold dough in half and seal edges. Place on lightly greased cookie sheets. Bake at 350° for 22 to 25 minutes. Sprinkle with confectioners' sugar, if desired.

Peekaberry Boos

2½ cups Pillsbury's Best All Purpose Flour
1 teaspoon soda
1 teaspoon salt
½ teaspoon cinnamon
1 cup firmly packed brown sugar
¾ cup sugar
½ cup butter
½ cup shortening
2 eggs
½ cup water
2 cups quick-cooking rolled oats
1 teaspoon almond extract
1 (12-ounce) jar red raspberry preserves

OVEN 400°   54 TO 60 COOKIES

In large mixer bowl combine all ingredients except preserves. Blend well.

Drop by rounded teaspoon onto ungreased cookie sheets. Make small indentation in center of each cookie and fill with ½ teaspoon preserves.

Bake at 400° for 10 to 12 minutes. Cool.

Cocoa Cheese Sandwich Cookies

2 cups Pillsbury's Best All Purpose Flour
½ teaspoon salt
¾ cup sugar
⅓ cup cocoa
¾ cup butter, softened
1 egg
1 teaspoon vanilla extract
Pecan halves

OVEN 350°   30 SANDWICH COOKIES

In large mixer bowl combine all ingredients except pecans. Blend well with mixer. Divide dough in half; shape into two 2-inch rolls. Wrap in waxed paper; chill at least 2 hours.

Cut into slices about ⅛-inch thick; place on ungreased cookie sheets. Garnish half the slices (for tops of sandwich cookies) with a small pecan half.

Bake at 350° for 8 to 10 minutes. Place two cookies together with Cheese Filling, sandwich style, using plain slices for bottoms.

Cheese Filling

Combine 3 tablespoons butter, softened; 1 tablespoon cream; 1 (3-ounce) package cream cheese, 2 cups confectioners' sugar and ¼ teaspoon salt. Mix thoroughly.

Mocha Mambos

1¾ cups Pillsbury's Best All Purpose Flour
½ teaspoon soda
½ teaspoon salt
 1 cup firmly packed brown sugar
¼ cup shortening
¼ cup butter, softened
 1 egg
¼ cup buttermilk
½ teaspoon vanilla
½ cup flaked coconut

OVEN 400°   30 TO 36 COOKIES

In large mixer bowl combine all ingredients except coconut. Blend well. Stir in coconut. Cover; chill for 1 hour.

Drop by rounded teaspoon onto ungreased cookie sheets. Bake at 400° for 7 to 10 minutes. Cool and cover tops completely with Fudge Frosting. Then drizzle with Coffee Glaze in zig-zag pattern.

Fudge Frosting

Prepare 1 package (small size) Pillsbury Buttercream Fudge Frosting Mix as directed on package.

Coffee Glaze

In small mixer bowl combine 1 teaspoon butter and ½ teaspoon instant coffee. Blend in ½ cup confectioners' sugar and gradually add 3 to 5 teaspoons hot water until the consistency of a glaze.

Pinwheel Butterflies

1¾ cups Pillsbury's Best All Purpose Flour
½ teaspoon baking powder
¼ teaspoon salt
¾ cup sugar
½ cup butter, softened
1 egg
1 teaspoon vanilla extract
1 teaspoon instant coffee
⅓ cup chopped pecans
1 (1-ounce) envelope premelted
  unsweetened chocolate

OVEN 350°   60 COOKIES

In large mixer bowl combine all ingredients except instant coffee, pecans and chocolate. Blend well with mixer.

Divide dough in half. Blend coffee and pecans to one half amount of dough. Add chocolate to remaining dough. Chill for easier handling.

Roll out light dough on waxed paper to a 16x8-inch rectangle. Repeat with chocolate dough. Place light dough on top chocolate dough. Roll up, starting with 16-inch side. Wrap in waxed paper; chill about 2 hours.

Cut into ¼-inch slices. Bake at 350° for 9 to 12 minutes.

Honey Candy Bites

½ cup butter
1 cup Pillsbury's Best All Purpose Flour
¼ teaspoon salt
¾ cup honey
2 tablespoons milk
1 teaspoon vanilla extract
1½ cups packaged grated coconut
2 cups rice crispy cereal or corn flakes,
  slightly crushed

42 TO 48 COOKIES

In large saucepan melt butter over low heat. Blend in flour, salt, honey and milk. Cook over medium heat, stirring constantly, until dough leaves sides of pan. Remove from heat. Stir in vanilla and 1 cup coconut. Cool. Add cereal.

Shape into 1-inch balls; roll in ½ cup coconut. Store in refrigerator.

Chocomint Creams

Crust:
½ cup butter
1 (1-ounce) envelope premelted
  unsweetened chocolate
1 cup Pillsbury's Best All Purpose Flour
½ cup confectioners' sugar

Filling:
1⅓ cups (15-ounce can) sweetened
  condensed milk
2 cups (7-ounce package) finely grated
  coconut
½ cup chopped pecans
36 solid chocolate mint candy wafers

OVEN 350°   36 SQUARES

In medium saucepan melt butter and chocolate over low heat, stirring constantly. Remove from heat. Add flour and sugar. Blend well. Press in greased 8-inch square pan. Bake at 350° for 10 to 12 minutes.

Combine milk, coconut and pecans. Spread carefully over partially baked crust. Bake at 350° for 25 to 30 minutes until filling is set.

Immediately place candy wafers on filling. Let stand 5 minutes. Spread chocolate evenly. Cool; cut into squares.

Chocolate Cherry Cheers

Mint Leaf Cookies

Honey Candy
Bites

Pinwheel Butterflies

Unbeatables

Chewy Coconut
Macaroons

Coconut
Honey Balls

Chocomint Creams

Lemon Larks

81

Unbeatables

2 cups confectioners' sugar
¾ cup Pillsbury's Best All Purpose Flour
½ teaspoon baking powder
½ cup (3 to 4) egg whites
2 cups chopped walnuts
½ cup chopped dried apricots

OVEN 325°   36 COOKIES

In large mixer bowl, combine sugar, flour, baking powder and egg whites. Blend well with mixer. Add walnuts and apricots; mix well. Drop by rounded teaspoons onto well-greased and floured cookie sheets. Bake at 325° for 15 to 18 minutes.

Variations:

Substitute 1 cup peanut butter pieces for the apricots.

Substitute 1 cup flaked coconut for the apricots. Add ⅛ teaspoon cinnamon and ⅛ teaspoon nutmeg with the flour.

Substitute 1 cup semi-sweet chocolate pieces for the apricots.

Chocolate Cherry Cheers

1 cup (6-ounce package) semi-sweet
   chocolate pieces
1 cup Pillsbury's Best All Purpose Flour
½ cup butter, softened
⅓ cup firmly packed brown sugar
36 maraschino cherries, well drained

OVEN 350°   36 SQUARES

In small saucepan melt chocolate pieces over low heat, stirring constantly. Remove from heat and set aside.

Combine flour, butter and sugar until well blended. Press in ungreased 8-inch square pan. Bake at 350° for 15 to 20 minutes. While warm cut in squares.

Arrange on waxed paper. Place a cherry on each square. Top with ½ teaspoon of chocolate. Let stand until chocolate hardens.

Lemon Larks

Cookie dough:
2 egg yolks
2 cups Pillsbury's Best All Purpose Flour
1 teaspoon baking powder
1 teaspoon salt
⅔ cup sugar
⅔ cup shortening
⅔ cup light cream
1 teaspoon prepared lemon peel
1 teaspoon prepared orange peel
1 tablespoon lemon juice

Meringue:
2 egg whites
¼ teaspoon cream of tartar
½ cup sugar

OVEN 350°   36 TO 42 COOKIES

In large mixer bowl combine all ingredients for cookie dough. Blend well with mixer. Drop by rounded teaspoon onto lightly greased cookie sheets.

Flatten cookies by pressing with bottom of glass which has been well greased, then dipped into sugar.

Prepare meringue by beating egg whites in small mixer bowl with cream of tartar until soft mounds form. Gradually add sugar and continue beating until meringue stands in stiff peaks. Place a rounded teaspoon of meringue on each cookie.

Bake at 350° for 15 to 18 minutes until delicately browned.

Chewy Coconut Macaroons

½ cup egg whites (4 medium)
1¼ cups sugar
½ cup Pillsbury's Best All Purpose Flour
¼ teaspoon salt
½ teaspoon vanilla extract
2½ cups (7-ounce package) flaked coconut

OVEN 325°   36 COOKIES

In large mixer bowl beat egg whites until soft mounds form. Gradually add ¼ cup sugar and beat until stiff peaks form. Fold in 1 cup sugar and remaining ingredients carefully, half at a time, until thoroughly blended.

Drop by rounded teaspoon onto greased and floured cookie sheets. Bake at 325° for 20 to 25 minutes until a delicate golden brown. Cool.

Coconut Honey Balls

2 cups Pillsbury's Best All Purpose Flour
½ cup sugar
1 cup butter, softened
1 teaspoon vanilla extract
1 teaspoon almond extract
1 cup chopped pecans
1 cup flaked coconut

OVEN 350°   70 TO 76 COOKIES

In large mixer bowl combine all ingredients except pecans and coconut. Blend well with mixer. Stir in remaining ingredients; mix thoroughly. Chill dough for easier handling.

Shape into balls using a teaspoon for each. Place on ungreased cookie sheets.

Bake at 350° for 15 to 18 minutes until a light golden brown. Cool. If desired, dip cookies into Glaze.

Glaze

Combine ¼ cup honey, ¼ cup apricot preserves and 1 tablespoon butter in saucepan. Simmer over low heat for 5 minutes. Remove from heat; cool.

Mint Leaf Cookies

4 eggs, separated
¾ cup sugar
1 teaspoon vanilla extract
¼ teaspoon salt
1 cup Pillsbury's Best All Purpose Flour

OVEN 350°   24 COOKIES

In small mixer bowl beat egg whites at high speed until soft peaks form. Gradually add ½ cup sugar; continue beating until stiff peaks form.

In large mixer bowl, combine egg yolks, ¼ cup sugar, vanilla extract and salt. Beat at high speed until very thick and lemon colored. Fold in beaten egg whites. Fold in flour gently but thoroughly.

Drop batter from side of teaspoon onto ungreased cookie sheet covered with brown paper, to resemble leaf shape. Sprinkle with sugar. Bake at 350° for 10 to 12 minutes. *Do not brown.* Cool before removing from paper. If necessary, slide flat knife under cookies to remove from paper. Place flat sides of 2 cookies together with Filling, sandwich-style.

Chocolate Mint Filling

1 (3-ounce) package cream cheese
2 tablespoons butter
2 cups confectioners' sugar
1 (1-ounce) envelope premelted
  unsweetened chocolate
1 tablespoon hot water
¼ teaspoon peppermint extract

In small mixing bowl combine cream cheese and butter. Blend well with mixer; gradually add sugar. Blend in chocolate, hot water and peppermint extract.

Peachadillies

I package Pillsbury Fluffy White Frosting
  Mix
I cup Pillsbury's Best All Purpose Flour
⅓ cup cooking oil
I cup (12-ounce jar) peach preserves
¼ teaspoon cinnamon
I cup finely chopped almonds

OVEN 350°   36 BARS

Preparing frosting mix as directed on package.
To half of frosting add flour and oil. Pat into
bottom of greased 13x9-inch pan.

Bake at 350° for 10 minutes. Spread with preserves.

Fold cinnamon and almonds into remaining
frosting; spread over preserves. Bake 25 to 30
minutes longer or until topping is golden
brown. Cool slightly. Cut into bars.

*Tip: If desired, other flavors of preserves may
be substituted.*

Brazilian Jubilee Cookies

1½ cups Pillsbury's Best All Purpose Flour
I to 2 tablespoons instant coffee
I teaspoon baking powder
½ teaspoon salt
½ teaspoon cinnamon
¾ cup sugar
¼ cup firmly packed brown sugar
½ cup shortening
I egg
2 teaspoons vanilla extract
I cup chopped Brazil nuts
  Solid milk chocolate candy kisses or
  semi-sweet chocolate pieces.

OVEN 350°   36 TO 42 COOKIES

In large mixer bowl combine all ingredients
except Brazil nuts and chocolate pieces. Blend
well with mixer. Stir in ½ cup Brazil nuts; mix
thoroughly. Chill dough for easier handling.

Shape into balls, using a rounded teaspoon
for each. Place on ungreased cookie sheets.
Bake at 350° for 12 to 15 minutes. Remove
from oven.

Press a candy kiss or 5 chocolate pieces into
center of each hot cookie. When chocolate
has softened, spread to frost. Sprinkle with
remaining chopped nuts.

Melt Away Bars

I egg, separated
2 cups Pillsbury's Best All Purpose Flour
I cup sugar
I cup butter, softened
I teaspoon vanilla extract
I cup chopped walnuts
  Colored sugar

OVEN 350°   40 BARS

In large mixer bowl combine egg yolk and remaining ingredients except walnuts and colored sugar. Blend well with mixer. Stir in ½
cup walnuts; mix thoroughly. Spread in ungreased 15x10x1-inch jelly roll pan.

Beat egg white until frothy; spread over bars.
Sprinkle with remaining walnuts and colored
sugar.

Bake at 350° for 25 to 30 minutes. Cool
slightly; cut into bars.

*Tip: ½ cup semi-sweet chocolate pieces and
½ cup peanut butter pieces may be sprinkled
over bars immediately after baking. Let stand
5 minutes; spread to form marble frosting.
Omit colored sugar.*
HIGH ALTITUDE ADJUSTMENT (5200 FEET)
Oven temperature 375°.

Starlight Mint Surprise Cookies

3 cups Pillsbury's Best All Purpose Flour
I teaspoon soda
½ teaspoon salt
I cup sugar
½ cup firmly packed brown sugar
I cup butter, softened
2 eggs
I teaspoon vanilla extract
2 (6½-ounce) packages chocolate mint
  candy wafers
  Walnut halves

OVEN 375°   54 COOKIES

Combine all ingredients except candy wafers
and walnuts in large mixer bowl. Blend well
with mixer.

Drop by scant teaspoon 2 inches apart onto
ungreased cookie sheets. Press candy wafer on
top of each. Cover with scant teaspoon of
dough. Top each with a walnut half; smooth
edges.

Bake at 375° for 9 to 12 minutes.

Butterscotch Pinwheels

Cookie dough:
* I cup (6-ounce package) semi-sweet chocolate pieces
* 2 tablespoons shortening
* I (15-ounce) can sweetened condensed milk
* I cup Pillsbury's Best All Purpose Flour
* I teaspoon vanilla extract
* ½ cup chopped walnuts

Butterscotch Filling:
* ! cup (6-ounce package) butterscotch pieces
* 2 tablespoons shortening

OVEN 325°   54 TO 60 COOKIES

In large saucepan melt chocolate pieces and shortening over low heat, stirring constantly. Remove from heat.

Add condensed milk, flour and vanilla extract. Blend well. Spread in 15x10x1-inch jelly roll pan which has been greased, lined with waxed paper and greased again. Bake at 325° for 8 minutes.

Prepare Butterscotch Filling while cookie dough is baking by melting butterscotch pieces with shortening in a small saucepan.

Immediately turn chocolate base onto a towel which has been sprinkled lightly with confectioners' sugar. Spread with Filling. Sprinkle with walnuts.

Roll up starting with 15-inch side. Wrap; store in refrigerator. Cut into ¼-inch slices.

Three Layer Party Squares

Crust:
* 2½ cups Pillsbury's Best All Purpose Flour
* I cup sugar
* ½ teaspoon salt
* I cup butter, softened
* 2 egg yolks
* I teaspoon vanilla extract
* I cup (6-ounce package) semi-sweet chocolate pieces

Meringue Topping:
* 2 egg whites
* ⅔ cup sugar
* ½ cup chopped walnuts

OVEN 375°   36 SQUARES

Walnut Sandwich Cookies

* 1½ cups Pillsbury's Best All Purpose Flour
* ½ teaspoon salt
* I cup sugar
* ¾ cup butter, softened
* I tablespoon water
* ¾ cup chopped walnuts

OVEN 350°   36 SANDWICH COOKIES

In large mixer bowl combine all ingredients. Blend well with mixer.

Shape into balls, using a scant teaspoon of dough for each. Place on ungreased cookie sheets. Flatten with a fork.

Bake at 350° for 12 to 15 minutes. Cool; place flat sides of two cookies together with Creamy Filling, sandwich-style. Brush tops with Orange Glaze.

Creamy Filling

Combine 1½ cups confectioners' sugar, I (3-ounce) package cream cheese, I tablespoon butter, softened and I teaspoon prepared orange peel. Beat until smooth.

Orange Glaze

Combine ¼ cup confectioners' sugar. I teaspoon prepared orange peel and I tablespoon orange juice. Mix well.

In large mixer bowl combine all ingredients for crust except chocolate pieces. Blend with mixer until particles are coarse crumbs. Press in greased 15x10x1-inch jelly roll pan. Bake at 375° for 15 to 20 minutes. Remove from oven and immediately sprinkle with chocolate pieces. Let stand 5 minutes. Spread over crust.

Prepare Meringue Topping by beating egg whites in small mixer bowl until soft mounds form. Gradually add remaining sugar and continue beating until stiff peaks form. Fold in walnuts.

Spread meringue carefully over chocolate, covering completely. Bake at 375° for 10 to 12 minutes. Cool; cut into squares.

Chocolate Nut Treasures

2½ cups Pillsbury's Best All Purpose Flour
1 teaspoon salt
½ teaspoon soda
1½ cups sugar
1 cup dairy sour cream
½ cup shortening
2 eggs
1 teaspoon vanilla extract
1 (1-ounce) envelope premelted
  unsweetened chocolate
½ cup chopped pecans
  Pecan halves, if desired

OVEN 400°   48 TO 54 COOKIES

In large mixer bowl combine all ingredients except chocolate and pecans. Blend well with mixer. Remove 1 cup of dough to small bowl; blend in chocolate and ½ cup pecans. Chill doughs at least 1 hour.

Drop light dough by teaspoon onto greased cookie sheets. Top each with a half teaspoon of chocolate dough.

Bake at 400° for 10 to 12 minutes. Cool and frost with Chocolate Frosting. Top with pecan half, if desired.

Chocolate Frosting

Prepare 1 package (small size) Pillsbury Buttercream Fudge Frosting Mix as directed on package.

Molasses Butter Crescents

1 cup butter, softened
⅓ cup molasses
2¼ cups Pillsbury's Best All Purpose Flour
2 cups finely chopped walnuts
¼ teaspoon salt
  Confectioners' sugar

OVEN 350°   54 TO 60 COOKIES

In large mixer bowl combine all ingredients except nuts and sugar. Blend well with mixer. Stir in walnuts; mix thoroughly. If desired, chill dough for easier handling.

Shape into crescents, using a rounded teaspoon for each. Place on ungreased cookie sheets. Bake at 350° for 12 to 15 minutes. Cool. Roll in confectioners' sugar.

Coconut Islands

2 cups Pillsbury's Best All Purpose Flour
½ teaspoon soda
½ teaspoon salt
1 teaspoon instant coffee
1 cup firmly packed brown sugar
½ cup butter, softened
1 egg
⅔ cup dairy sour cream
3 (1-ounce) envelopes premelted
  unsweetened chocolate
1 cup flaked coconut

OVEN 375°   42 TO 48 COOKIES

In large mixer bowl combine all ingredients except ⅔ cup of coconut. Blend well with mixer.

Drop by rounded teaspoon onto greased cookie sheets.

Bake at 375° for 12 to 15 minutes. Frost while warm. Sprinkle with remaining ⅔ cup coconut.

Chocolate Frosting

Combine 2 (1-ounce) envelopes premelted unsweetened chocolate, ¼ cup dairy sour cream and 2 cups confectioners' sugar in a small mixer bowl. Blend well. If necessary, thin with a few drops of cream or milk.

Boutonnieres

2 cups Pillsbury's Best All Purpose Flour
2 teaspoons baking powder
¾ teaspoon salt
1½ cups firmly packed brown sugar
1 cup butter, softened
1 egg
1 teaspoon vanilla extract
1½ cups quick-cooking rolled oats
1 cup chopped walnuts
1 cup flaked coconut

OVEN 350°   66 TO 72 COOKIES

In large mixer bowl combine all ingredients except rolled oats, walnuts and coconut. Blend well with mixer. Stir in remaining ingredients; mix thoroughly.

Drop by rounded teaspoon onto ungreased cookie sheets. Bake at 350° for 12 to 15 minutes until golden brown.

HIGH ALTITUDE ADJUSTMENT (5200 FEET)
Oven temperature 375°. Decrease baking powder to 1½ teaspoons.

Malted Mocha Dreams

Crust:
  1¾ cups Pillsbury's Best All Purpose Flour
  ¾ cup butter, softened
  ⅔ cup firmly packed brown sugar

Topping:
  ¼ cup Pillsbury's Best All Purpose Flour
  ¾ cup instant chocolate malted milk powder
  ½ cup sugar
   1 teaspoon baking powder
  ¼ teaspoon salt
   3 eggs
   2 teaspoons vanilla extract
   1 cup flaked coconut
   1 cup chopped pecans

OVEN 350°   36 BARS

Combine all ingredients for crust in large mixer bowl. Blend with mixer until particles are fine. Press in ungreased 13x9-inch pan. Bake at 350° for 10 minutes.

In same large mixer bowl combine all ingredients for topping except coconut and pecans. Blend well. Stir in coconut and pecans; mix thoroughly. Spread over partially baked crust.

Bake at 350° for 25 to 30 minutes. Cool and frost with Mocha-Malt Frosting. Cut in bars.

Mocha-Malt Frosting

   3 tablespoons instant chocolate malted
     milk powder
  ½ teaspoon instant coffee
   2 tablespoons hot water
   2 tablespoons butter, softened
   1 teaspoon vanilla extract
  1½ cups confectioners' sugar

In small mixer bowl combine malted milk powder, instant coffee and hot water. Blend well with mixer. Add butter, vanilla and confectioners' sugar. Beat until smooth, thinning with a few drops of water if necessary, until of spreading consistency.

Malted Mocha Dreams

Coconut Islands

Molasses Butter Crescents

Starlight Mint Surprise Cookies

Three Layer Party Squares

Brazilian Jubilee Cookies

Wa
Sandw
Coo

Butterscotch Pinwheels

Chocolate Nut Treasures

Melt Away Bars

Peachadillies

Boutonnieres

Peanut Quickies

Candy Bar Brownies

Banana Bonanza Cookies

Butterscotch Coconut D

Banana Bonanza Cookies

2⅔ cups Pillsbury's Best All Purpose Flour
¼ teaspoon salt
 1 cup confectioners' sugar
 1 cup butter, softened
⅓ cup (1 small) banana
½ teaspoon vanilla extract
½ cup chopped almonds

OVEN 350°   36 SANDWICH COOKIES

In large mixer bowl combine all ingredients. Blend well. Chill dough for easier handling.

Shape into balls using rounded teaspoon for each. Place on ungreased cookie sheets. Flatten with bottom of glass dipped in sugar.

Bake at 350° for 10 to 12 minutes. Cool; place flat sides of two cookies together with Cream Cheese Filling, sandwich-style.

Cream Cheese Filling

Soften 1 (3-ounce) package cream cheese. Blend in 1 cup confectioners' sugar and 2 tablespoons chopped maraschino cherries.

Tip: to keep cookies crisp, store Filling in refrigerator and fill cookies just before serving.

Peanut Quickies

 1 package Pillsbury Fluffy White
   Frosting Mix
½ cup Pillsbury's Best All Purpose Flour
½ cup crunchy peanut butter

OVEN 375°   42 TO 48 COOKIES

Prepare frosting mix as directed on package. Fold in flour, then peanut butter. Drop dough by rounded teaspoon onto greased and floured cookie sheets.

Bake at 375° for 10 to 12 minutes until golden. Remove from cookie sheets immediately. Cool.

Tip: If desired, ½ cup salted peanuts may be added to dough.

Butterscotch Coconut Drops

 2 cups Pillsbury's Best All Purpose Flour
½ teaspoon soda
½ teaspoon salt
½ cup firmly packed brown sugar
½ cup sugar
½ cup butter, softened
 2 eggs
 1 teaspoon vanilla extract
 1 cup (6-ounce package) butterscotch
   pieces
½ cup chopped walnuts
   Flaked coconut

OVEN 375°   54 TO 60 COOKIES

In large mixer bowl combine all ingredients except butterscotch pieces, walnuts and coconut. Blend well with mixer. Stir in butterscotch pieces and walnuts; mix thoroughly. Chill dough at least 1 hour.

Shape into balls using a rounded teaspoon for each. Dip tops in coconut. Place on ungreased cookie sheets. If desired, top with maraschino cherries or pecan halves.

Bake at 375° for 10 to 12 minutes. Cool.

Candy Bar Brownies

 2 chocolate-covered coconut candy bars
   (4 sections)
½ cup shortening
 1 cup Pillsbury's Best All Purpose Flour
 1 cup sugar
½ teaspoon salt
 2 eggs
 1 teaspoon vanilla extract
½ cup chopped walnuts

OVEN 350°   36 BARS

In large saucepan melt candy bars and shortening over low heat, stirring constantly. Remove from heat. Add remaining ingredients and blend well. Spread in greased 9-inch square pan.

Bake at 350° for 25 to 30 minutes. While warm cut into bars.

Hoosier Peanut Bars

Crust:
    2 cups Pillsbury's Best All Purpose Flour
    1 teaspoon soda
    ½ teaspoon salt
    ½ cup butter, softened
    ½ cup sugar
    ½ cup firmly packed brown sugar
    2 egg yolks
    1 teaspoon vanilla extract

Topping:
    2 egg whites
    1 cup firmly packed brown sugar
    1 cup (6-ounce package) semi-sweet
      chocolate pieces
    1 cup chopped salted peanuts

OVEN 325°   36 BARS

In large mixer bowl combine all ingredients for crust. Blend with mixer until particles are fine. Press in a greased 13x9-inch pan.

To prepare topping beat egg whites in small mixer bowl until soft mounds form. Add brown sugar gradually and continue beating until meringue stands in stiff peaks. Fold in chocolate pieces and ½ cup peanuts. Spread over crumb crust and sprinkle with remaining peanuts.

Bake at 325° for 40 to 45 minutes. While warm, cut into bars.
HIGH ALTITUDE ADJUSTMENT (5200 FEET)
Oven temperature 350°. Decrease soda to ¾ teaspoon.

Nutty Fudge-wiches

    ½ cup butter, softened
    1½ cups Pillsbury's Best All Purpose Flour
    1½ cups firmly packed brown sugar
    ¾ cup chopped walnuts
    1 teaspoon baking powder
    ¼ teaspoon salt
    1 teaspoon vanilla extract
    3 eggs
    2 (1-ounce) envelopes premelted
      unsweetened chocolate
    1 (8-ounce) package cream cheese

OVEN 350°   24 BARS

In large mixing bowl, combine butter, flour, 1 cup sugar, ½ cup walnuts, baking powder, salt, vanilla extract, eggs, chocolate and half of cream cheese. Mix until smooth and well blended, about 1 minute. Spread about half of mixture in greased 9-inch square pan.

Blend remaining cream cheese with ½ cup sugar. Spread carefully over batter in pan.

Top with other half of chocolate mixture, spreading carefully to cover. Sprinkle with ¼ cup walnuts.

Bake at 350° for 25 to 30 minutes. Cool. Cut into bars.

Surfer Squares

    1 cup (6-ounce package) butterscotch
      pieces
    ¼ cup granulated brown sugar
    ¼ cup butter
    1 egg
    ¾ cup Pillsbury's Best All Purpose Flour
    1 teaspoon baking powder
    ¼ teaspoon salt
    1 cup (6-ounce package) semi-sweet
      chocolate pieces
    1 cup miniature marshmallows
    ½ cup chopped walnuts
    1 teaspoon vanilla extract

OVEN 350°   24 BARS

In large saucepan melt butterscotch pieces, sugar and butter over medium heat, stirring constantly. Remove from heat. Add egg; beat well. Add flour, baking powder and salt. Stir in remaining ingredients.

Spread in greased 8-inch square pan. Bake at 350° for 20 to 25 minutes. Cool; cut into bars.

Nutty Fudge-wiches

Hoosier Peanut Bars

Jim Dandies

Snappy Turtle Cookies

Surfer Squares

93

Jim Dandies

1½ cups Pillsbury's Best All Purpose Flour
½ teaspoon soda
½ teaspoon salt
⅔ cup firmly packed brown sugar
½ cup shortening
  1 egg
⅓ cup maraschino cherry liquid
  2 (1-ounce) envelopes premelted
    unsweetened chocolate
½ cup chopped walnuts
¼ cup maraschino cherries, drained and
    chopped
18 marshmallows, cut in half or 1 cup
    miniature marshmallows
36 walnut halves

OVEN 350°   36 COOKIES

In large mixer bowl combine all ingredients except walnuts, cherries, marshmallows and walnut halves. Blend well. Stir in chopped walnuts and cherries.

Drop by rounded teaspoon onto ungreased cookie sheets. Bake at 350° for 10 to 12 minutes.

While hot, top each cookie with a marshmallow half or 3 miniature marshmallows. Remove from cookie sheets. Cool; frost and top with a walnut half.

Double Dutch Fudge Frosting

Prepare 1 package (regular size) Pillsbury Double Dutch Fudge Buttercream Frosting Mix as directed on package.

Snappy Turtle Cookies*

1½ cups Pillsbury's Best All Purpose Flour
¼ teaspoon soda
¼ teaspoon salt
½ cup firmly packed brown sugar
½ cup butter, softened
  1 egg and 1 egg yolk (reserve white)
¼ teaspoon vanilla extract
⅛ teaspoon maple flavoring
  2 cups pecan halves

OVEN 350°   24 TO 30 COOKIES

In large mixer bowl combine all ingredients except pecans. Blend well with mixer. Chill dough.

Arrange pecan halves in groups of three or five on greased cookie sheets to resemble head and legs of a turtle. Shape dough into balls, using a rounded teaspoon for each. Dip bottom of ball into unbeaten egg white; press lightly onto nuts. Be sure tips of pecans will show when cookie is baked.

Bake at 350° for 10 to 12 minutes. Do not overbake. Cool; frost tops generously.

Chocolate Frosting

Prepare 1 package (small size) Pillsbury Buttercream Fudge Frosting Mix as directed on package.

Not to be confused with "Turtles" brand candies made exclusively by De Met's Inc. of Chicago, Illinois.

Walnut Walkaways

 1 package active dry yeast
 1/4 cup warm water
 2 cups Pillsbury's Best All Purpose Flour
 1/8 teaspoon salt
 3/4 cup butter
 1 egg
 1 (3-ounce) package cream cheese,
   softened
 1/2 cup sugar
 1 teaspoon prepared orange peel
 1 teaspoon prepared lemon peel
 1/2 cup finely chopped walnuts
   Confectioners' sugar

OVEN 375°   24 COOKIES

Soften yeast in warm water. Combine flour and salt in mixing bowl. Cut in butter until mixture resembles coarse crumbs. Add yeast and egg; mix just until blended.

Roll out dough, half at a time, on floured surface to a 13x9-inch rectangle.

Beat cream cheese, sugar and orange and lemon peels until light and fluffy. Spread half on each rectangle; sprinkle with walnuts. Starting with 13-inch side, roll up jelly roll fashion. Place on lightly greased cookie sheet, seamside down. Cut each roll halfway through lengthwise.

Bake at 375° for 20 to 25 minutes. Cool. Sprinkle with confectioners' sugar. Cut diagonally into 1-inch slices.

Oriental Tea Treats

 2 1/2 cups Pillsbury's Best All Purpose Flour
 1/2 teaspoon soda
 1/4 teaspoon salt
 1 3/4 cups firmly packed brown sugar
 1/2 cup butter, softened
 1/2 cup shortening
 1/4 cup water
 1 cup chopped almonds
 1/4 cup crystallized ginger, finely chopped

OVEN 350°   60 TO 66 COOKIES

In large mixer bowl combine all ingredients, except almonds and ginger. Blend well with mixer. Stir in remaining ingredients; mix thoroughly.

Shape into balls using a rounded teaspoon for each. Place on ungreased cookie sheets.

Bake at 350° for 12 to 15 minutes. Cool.

Peanut Sticks

 1 3/4 cups Pillsbury's Best All Purpose Flour
 1/2 cup confectioners' sugar
 1/4 cup firmly packed brown sugar
 3/4 cup butter, softened
 1 teaspoon vanilla extract
 1 cup chopped salted peanuts

OVEN 350°   48 TO 54 COOKIES

In large mixer bowl combine all ingredients except peanuts. Blend well. Stir in 1/2 cup peanuts; mix thoroughly.

Shape into sticks 10 inches long and 1/2 inch in diameter. Cut into 2-inch sticks. Place on ungreased cookie sheets. Bake at 350° for 12 to 15 minutes. Cool.

Frost with Coffee Frosting and sprinkle with remaining 1/2 cup peanuts.

Coffee Frosting

In small mixer bowl combine 2 tablespoons butter, softened, 1 cup confectioners' sugar, 1 teaspoon instant coffee and 1/2 teaspoon vanilla extract. Blend in 1 to 2 tablespoons milk until of spreading consistency.

Sesame Bars

 1/2 cup butter
 1 cup sesame seed
 1 1/4 cups Pillsbury's Best All Purpose Flour
 1 (15-ounce) can sweetened condensed
   milk
 1/2 cup evaporated or whole milk
 1 teaspoon vanilla extract

                         16 BARS

In heavy skillet melt butter over medium heat. Add sesame seed, stirring and cooking until golden brown, about 5 minutes.

Add flour, continue stirring; until golden brown. Remove from heat.

Add remaining ingredients; mix well. Cook over medium heat, stirring constantly until mixture is glossy and leaves sides of pan, about 3 minutes. Pat into 8-inch square pan. Cool, then refrigerate. Cut into bars, squares or triangles.

Walnut Walkaways

Oriental Treasure Cookies

Sugar Cheese
Crescents

Oriental
Tea Treats

Sesame
Bars

Macaroon
Toppers

Peanut Sticks

Apricot Jewels

Oriental Treasure Cookies

Cookie dough:
  1⅔ cups Pillsbury's Best All Purpose Flour
  1½ teaspoons baking powder
  ½ teaspoon soda
  ½ cup firmly packed brown sugar
  ½ cup sugar
  ½ cup shortening
  I egg
  I tablespoon soy sauce
  ½ teaspoon almond extract
Almond Topping:
  ½ cup slivered almonds
  2 teaspoons sugar
  I teaspoon soy sauce

OVEN 350°   46 TO 50 COOKIES

In large mixer bowl combine all ingredients. Blend well with mixer. Shape into balls, using a rounded teaspoon for each.

Combine all ingredients for almond topping. Dip top of cookies into almond mixture. Place on ungreased cookie sheets.

Bake at 350° for 12 to 15 minutes.
HIGH ALTITUDE ADJUSTMENT (5200 FEET)
Oven temperature 375°. Decrease baking powder to I teaspoon.

Apricot Jewels

  1¼ cups Pillsbury's Best All Purpose Flour
  1½ teaspoons baking powder
  ¼ teaspoon salt
  ¼ cup sugar
  ½ cup butter, softened
  I (3-ounce) package cream cheese, softened
  ½ cup flaked coconut
  ½ cup apricot preserves

OVEN 350°   30 TO 36 COOKIES

In large mixer bowl combine all ingredients except coconut and preserves. Blend with mixer until particles are coarse. Stir in coconut and preserves. Mix thoroughly.

Drop by teaspoon onto ungreased cookie sheets. Bake at 350° for 15 to 18 minutes until lightly browned. Frost with Apricot Frosting while warm. If desired, decorate with nut half or flaked coconut.

Apricot Frosting

Combine I cup confectioners' sugar with I tablespoon softened butter and ¼ cup apricot preserves. Beat until smooth.
HIGH ALTITUDE ADJUSTMENT (5200 FEET)
Oven temperature 375° Decrease baking powder to I teaspoon. Decrease baking time to 13 to 15 minutes.

Macaroon Toppers

Cookie dough:
  1¼ cups Pillsbury's Best All Purpose Flour
  ¼ teaspoon salt
  ½ cup firmly packed brown sugar
  ½ cup butter, softened
  I egg yolk
  ½ teaspoon vanilla extract
Coconut Topping:
  2⅔ cups (7-ounce package) flaked coconut
  ½ cup confectioners' sugar
  I egg white
  I tablespoon water
  ½ teaspoon vanilla extract

OVEN 375°   36 TO 42 COOKIES

In large mixer bowl combine all ingredients for cookie dough. Blend well with mixer. Form into a 10-inch roll. Wrap in waxed paper and chill about I hour.

Combine all ingredients for Coconut Topping. Chill.

Cut cookie dough in ¼-inch slices. Place on ungreased cookie sheets. Top with rounded teaspoon coconut topping.

Bake at 375° for 12 to 15 minutes until golden brown.

Tip: Cut maraschino or candied cherries in sixths. Place one on each cookie.

Sugar Cheese Crescents

  I cup sugar
  2½ cups Pillsbury's Best All Purpose Flour
  ½ teaspoon salt
  ¾ cup butter, softened
  ⅓ cup sweetened applesauce
  ½ teaspoon vanilla extract
  ½ cup shredded Cheddar cheese
  I teaspoon cinnamon

OVEN 350°   50 TO 56 COOKIES

In large mixer bowl combine ½ cup sugar and remaining ingredients except cheese and cinnamon. Blend well. Stir in cheese; mix thoroughly.

Shape into balls using a rounded teaspoon of dough for each. Roll each ball in a mixture of ½ cup sugar and cinnamon. Press with tines of a fork or mold into crescent shapes. Place on ungreased cookie sheets.

Bake at 350° for 12 to 15 minutes. Remove from cookie sheets immediately.

Choco-Peanut Toppers

Crisp Lemon Thins

Rise'n Shiners

Chocolate Pixies

Peanut Shorties

Nut Cluster Cookies

Crisp Lemon Thins

¾ cup Pillsbury's Best All Purpose Flour
¾ cup firmly packed brown sugar
½ cup butter, softened
  1 egg
  1 tablespoon prepared lemon peel
½ teaspoon lemon extract
½ cup finely chopped almonds
¼ cup quick-cooking rolled oats

OVEN 350°   36 TO 42 COOKIES

In large mixer bowl combine all ingredients except almonds and rolled oats. Blend well with mixer. Stir in remaining ingredients; mix thoroughly.

Drop by scant teaspoon onto greased and floured or teflon cookie sheets. Bake at 350° for 7 to 10 minutes until edges are golden brown. Remove from cookie sheets immediately.

Peanut Shorties

2 cups Pillsbury's Best All Purpose Flour
  1 teaspoon soda
½ teaspoon salt
  1 cup peanut butter
½ cup butter, softened
  1 cup firmly packed brown sugar
½ cup sugar
  2 eggs
  1 teaspoon vanilla extract
  1 cup coarsely chopped cocktail peanuts

OVEN 350°   54 TO 60 COOKIES

In large mixer bowl combine all ingredients except peanuts. Blend well. Chill for easier handling.

Roll out dough, half at a time, on floured surface to ⅛-inch thickness. Cut into rounds with floured 2½-inch cutter. Place on ungreased cookie sheets. Bake at 350° for 8 to 10 minutes. Let stand 1 minute; remove from sheets.

Top each cookie with a teaspoon of peanuts. Drizzle with a teaspoon of Praline Frosting. If frosting thickens, thin with a few drops of cream.

Praline Frosting

Combine 1 cup firmly packed brown sugar and ½ cup cream in small saucepan. Cook, stirring constantly, until mixture comes to a boil; boil 2 minutes. Cool slightly and blend in 2 cups confectioners' sugar.
HIGH ALTITUDE ADJUSTMENT (5200 FEET)
Oven temperature 375°. Decrease soda to ¾ teaspoon and sugar to ⅓ cup.

98

Choco-Peanut Toppers

2 cups Pillsbury's Best All Purpose Flour
I cup butter, softened
½ cup sugar
2 teaspoons vanilla extract

OVEN 325°   54 TO 60 COOKIES

In large mixer bowl combine all ingredients and blend well. Drop by level teaspoon onto greased cookie sheets. Flatten to ¼-inch with glass, greased on the bottom then dipped in sugar.

Bake at 325° for I5 to I8 minutes. Spread warm cookies with Peanut Butter Topping. Drizzle with Chocolate Glaze. Let stand until Glaze is set.

Peanut Butter Topping

Cream ¼ cup butter with ⅓ cup firmly packed brown sugar and ⅓ cup peanut butter until light and fluffy.

Chocolate Glaze

Melt ½ cup semi-sweet chocolate pieces with 2 tablespoons milk in a saucepan over low heat, stirring constantly. Remove from heat. Add ⅓ cup sifted confectioners' sugar; stir until smooth.

Nut Cluster Cookies

I¼ cups Pillsbury's Best All Purpose Flour
¼ teaspoon salt
¼ teaspoon cream of tartar
¼ teaspoon soda
½ cup sugar
⅓ cup shortening
 I egg
2 tablespoons milk
 I teaspoon vanilla extract
½ cup chopped salted peanuts

OVEN 375°   30 TO 36 COOKIES

In large mixer bowl combine all ingredients except peanuts. Blend well with mixer. Stir in peanuts; mix thoroughly.

Drop by teaspoon onto ungreased cookie sheets. Bake at 375° for 8 to I0 minutes. Cool. Top with Chocolate Glaze.

Chocolate Glaze

Prepare I package (small size) Pillsbury Butter-cream Fudge Frosting Mix as directed on package and increasing water to 3 tablespoons.

Rise 'n Shiners

Cookie dough:
2¼ cups Pillsbury's Best All Purpose Flour
½ teaspoon salt
¾ cup butter, softened
½ cup light cream
 I package active dry yeast
 I teaspoon almond extract

Cereal-Nut Topping:
½ cup firmly packed brown sugar
 I cup chopped pecans
⅓ cup crushed corn flakes
½ cup chopped maraschino cherries
¼ cup melted butter

OVEN 350°   30 COOKIES

In large mixer bowl combine flour, salt and butter. Blend until particles are fine. Combine remaining cookie dough ingredients; stir into flour mixture to form a dough.

Roll out on floured surface to a I2x10-inch rectangle. Let stand while preparing cereal-nut topping.

Combine all topping ingredients; blend well.

Spread dough with topping, pressing firmly into dough. Cut into 2-inch squares; place on ungreased cookie sheets.

Bake at 350° for 25 to 30 minutes. Cool.

Chocolate Pixies

4 (I-ounce) envelopes premelted
    unsweetened chocolate
¼ cup butter
2 cups Pillsbury's Best All Purpose Flour
2 teaspoons baking powder
½ teaspoon salt
2 cups sugar
3 eggs
½ cup chopped walnuts
    Confectioners' sugar

OVEN 300°   48 TO 54 COOKIES

In large saucepan melt chocolate and butter over low heat, stirring constantly. Remove from heat. Cool slightly. Stir in remaining ingredients, except confectioners' sugar. Blend well. Chill at least 30 minutes.

Shape into balls using a rounded teaspoon for each. Roll in confectioners' sugar. Place on greased cookie sheets.

Bake at 300° for I8 to 20 minutes. Cool.

Macaroonies

Chocolate
Press Cookies

Butter Crunch Slices

Peanut Whirligigs

Chocolate Press Cookies

    2 cups Pillsbury's Best All Purpose Flour
    ½ teaspoon salt
    1 cup sugar
    ½ cup butter, softened
    2 (1-ounce) envelopes premelted
       unsweetened chocolate
    2 tablespoons milk
    1 egg
    1 teaspoon vanilla extract

OVEN 350°   70 TO 76 COOKIES

In large mixer bowl combine all ingredients. Blend well with mixer.

Press a small amount of dough through a cookie press onto ungreased cookie sheets, using any plate to make desired shape.

Bake at 350° for 6 to 9 minutes.

Peanut Whirligigs

Cookie dough:
    ½ cup butter, softened
    2 cups Pillsbury's Best All Purpose Flour
    ½ teaspoon salt
    1 cup sugar ·
    ½ cup shortening
    1 (3-ounce) package cream cheese,
       softened
    1 teaspoon vanilla extract
    ¾ cup finely chopped salted peanuts

Chocolate Filling:
    ¼ cup butter
    1 cup (6-ounce package) semi-sweet
       chocolate pieces

OVEN 375°   66 TO 72 COOKIES

In large mixer bowl combine all ingredients for cookie dough except peanuts. Blend well with mixer. Stir in peanuts; mix thoroughly. Chill dough for easier handling.

In a small saucepan melt filling ingredients over low heat, stirring constantly. Remove from heat. Cool slightly.

Roll out half of dough on a floured surface to a 16x9-inch rectangle. Spread half of chocolate over rolled dough in a thin layer. Roll up starting with the 9-inch side. Wrap in waxed paper. Repeat with remaining dough and chocolate. Chill at least 2 hours or overnight.

Cut into slices ⅛-inch thick. Place on ungreased cookie sheets. Bake at 375° for 7 to 10 minutes. Cool 1 minute before removing from cookie sheets.

Macaroonies

     2 eggs
    ⅛ teaspoon salt
    ¾ cup sugar
    ½ cup Pillsbury's Best All Purpose Flour
    1 tablespoon butter, melted
    2 cups flaked coconut
    1 cup (6-ounce package) semi-sweet
       chocolate pieces
    1 teaspoon prepared orange peel
    1 teaspoon vanilla extract

OVEN 325°   38 TO 44 COOKIES

Beat eggs with salt until foamy in small mixer bowl. Gradually add sugar; continue beating until thick. Fold in flour and butter. Stir in remaining ingredients.

Drop by rounded teaspoon onto lightly greased and floured cookie sheets.

Bake at 325° for 12 to 15 minutes until delicately browned. Cool.

Butter Crunch Slices

Filling:
    1 cup (6-ounce package) butterscotch
       pieces, melted
    1 cup finely chopped salted peanuts
    ¼ cup peanut butter
    ⅓ cup sweetened condensed milk
    1 tablespoon butter, softened
    1 teaspoon vanilla extract

Cookie dough:
    ¼ cup peanut butter
    ½ cup butter, softened
    1 cup Pillsbury's Best All Purpose Flour
    ½ cup sugar
    ½ teaspoon salt
    ½ cup quick-cooking rolled oats

OVEN 350°   70 TO 76 COOKIES

Combine all ingredients for filling. Chill while preparing cookie dough.

In large mixer bowl combine ingredients for cookie dough. Blend well with mixer.

Divide dough in half. Pat out each half to a 12x6-inch rectangle on waxed paper. Spoon filling down center of each rectangle. Roll dough around filling. Wrap; chill at least 2 hours.

Cut into ¼-inch slices. Place on ungreased cookie sheets. Bake at 350° for 12 to 15 minutes. Cool 1 minute before removing from cookie sheets.

Holiday Cookies

• Holidays are traditional cookie baking times and everyone has carefully treasured favorites they bake each year to tuck in gift packages or serve when friends drop in. In this section we've included some of the popular Christmas cookies as well as some new ones to add to your collection.

If you want to give your Christmas tree an old-fashioned look decorate it with cut-out cookie snow men, santas, wreaths or other shapes. To fasten to the tree, cut a 3 to 4-inch length of clean string and press about I inch into the back of each cookie before baking. Or with a skewer make a hole ½ inch from the top of the cookie before baking so a ribbon or thread may be inserted afterwards to loop over the tree branch.

A gaily wrapped gift of Christmas cookies for the helpful neighbor, the postman or the children's teacher would be a welcome treat. In many European countries it is customary to take a gift of cookies when visiting at Christmas time. Empty coffee cans wrapped in colored foil or small wicker baskets make ideal containers. Wrap in clear plastic or red or green cellophane and fasten with a bright crisp bow with a sprig of holly. Hand carried gifts may include any number and variety of cookies. But if they are to be mailed, choose them from the less fragile varieties and refer to page 48 for hints on packing and shipping.

Many communities have an annual cookie exchange or bake sale during the holidays. It's an opportunity to add to the variety you have without making as many batches. Pick your favorites to bake and watch them disappear when they're put on display.

Christmas is a time when you usually make extra effort to decorate cookies. Use a fondant type frosting that dries quickly for cookies you intend to pack. Candied cherry pieces, citron, nuts, red hot candies and colored sugars will add to the Christmas spirit. The cake and frosting decorator in holiday red and green with the four different tips greatly speeds the decorating project.

Whichever recipes you choose we hope they make your Christmas baking merry.

Brazil Nut
Refrigerator Slices

Bake-Me-Not Peanut Bars

Oatmeal Carmelitas

Cherry-Nut Sli

Golden Pear Drops

Sunshine Dream Bars

Date-Nut Ribbons

Licorice Snaps

Date-Nut Ribbons

Cookie Dough:
    2 cups Pillsbury's Best All Purpose Flour
  ½ teaspoon salt
  ¼ teaspoon soda
   1 cup firmly packed brown sugar
  ½ cup shortening
   1 tablespoon milk
   1 egg
Date-Nut Filling:
   1 (12-ounce) can date cake and pastry filling
   1 tablespoon lemon juice
  ½ cup chopped walnuts

OVEN 350°   48 TO 56 COOKIES

In large mixer bowl combine all ingredients for Cookie Dough. Blend well with mixer. Chill at least 1 hour.

Combine ingredients for Date-Nut Filling and mix well.

Roll out dough on floured surface to a 14x8-inch rectangle. Cut in half cross-wise. Cut each half into four 2-inch strips. Spread Date Filling on 6 strips. Make 2 stacks of 4 strips, placing plain strip on top. Wrap; chill at least 3 hours. Cut into ¼-inch slices. Place on ungreased cookie sheets. Bake at 350° for 12 to 15 minutes. Cool slightly before removing from cookie sheets.

Tip: If date cake and pastry filling is not available prepare Date-Nut Filling by combining in saucepan 1¼ cups (8-ounce) package chopped dates, ½ cup chopped walnuts, ½ cup sugar, ½ cup water and 1 tablespoon lemon juice. Cook over low heat, stirring constantly until thickened, 5 to 6 minutes. Cool.

Bake-Me-Not Peanut Bars

   1 cup butter, softened
  ⅓ cup creamy peanut butter
1½ cups Pillsbury's Best All Purpose Flour
   1 teaspoon vanilla extract
  ¾ cup cocktail peanuts
   2 cups sugar
   1 cup water   24 BARS

In large mixer bowl combine all ingredients except sugar and water. Blend well with mixer.

In 1½-quart saucepan, cook sugar and water to hard-ball stage (250° F.), or until syrup forms a hard ball when dropped into very cold water. Pour slowly over butter-flour mixture. Stir until thickened and well blended. Pour into buttered 11x7-inch pan. Cool. Cut into bars.

Licorice Snaps

2½ cups Pillsbury's Best All Purpose Flour
   1 cup sugar
   1 cup firmly packed brown sugar
   1 teaspoon soda
  ½ teaspoon salt
  ½ teaspoon cloves
  ½ teaspoon cinnamon
   1 cup butter, softened
   1 egg
   1 tablespoon anise seed
  ½ cup chopped pecans

OVEN 375°   78 TO 84 COOKIES

In large mixer bowl combine all ingredients. Blend well with mixer. Divide dough in half. Shape into two 10-inch rolls. Wrap in waxed paper. Chill at least 4 hours.

Cut into ¼-inch slices. Place on ungreased cookie sheets. Bake at 375° for 10 to 12 minutes.

Brazil Nut Refrigerator Slices

   2 cups Pillsbury's Best All Purpose Flour
  ½ teaspoon soda
  ½ teaspoon salt
   1 cup sugar
  ½ cup butter, softened
   1 egg
   1 tablespoon molasses
  ½ cup flaked coconut
  ½ cup chopped Brazil nuts

OVEN 375°   72 TO 78 COOKIES

In large mixer bowl combine all ingredients except coconut and Brazil nuts. Blend well with mixer. Stir in remaining ingredients; mix thoroughly.

Divide dough into two parts. Place on waxed paper and shape into rolls 1½ inches in diameter. Chill 1 hour if desired.

Cut into ⅛-inch slices with a sharp knife. Place on ungreased cookie sheets.

Bake at 375° for 8 to 10 minutes.

Cherry-Nut Slices

2¼ cups Pillsbury All Purpose Flour
  1 cup butter or margarine, softened
  1 egg
  2 tablespoons milk
  1 teaspoon vanilla
  1 cup confectioners' sugar
  2 cups candied cherries
  1 cup pecan halves

OVEN 400°   80 COOKIES

In large mixer bowl, combine all ingredients except cherries and nuts. Blend well at low speed. Stir in cherries and nuts; mix thoroughly. If necessary, chill 1 hour. Shape dough into two 10-inch rolls; wrap. Chill 1 to 2 hours. Cut into ¼-inch slices. Place on ungreased cookie sheets. Bake at 400° for 7 to 10 minutes. Cool.

Sunshine Dream Bars

Crust:
  1 cup Pillsbury's Best All Purpose Flour
⅓ cup sugar
  2 teaspoons prepared lemon peel
¼ cup butter, softened
¼ cup (2 ounces) cream cheese, softened

Lemon Cheese Filling:
¾ cup (6 ounces) cream cheese, softened
⅓ cup sugar
  2 eggs
  1 teaspoon prepared lemon peel
  2 tablespoons lemon juice

Golden Nut Topping:
  2 tablespoons Pillsbury's Best All Purpose
      Flour
  1 teaspoon baking powder
½ teaspoon salt
  1 cup firmly packed brown sugar
  2 eggs
  1 teaspoon vanilla extract
  1 cup chopped walnuts

OVEN 350°   36 BARS

In large mixer bowl combine all ingredients for crust. Blend with mixer until particles are fine. Press in well-greased 13x9-inch pan. Bake at 350° for 12 to 15 minutes until light brown.

Combine all ingredients for Filling in small mixer bowl. Blend well. Pour Filling over partially baked crust.

In same small mixer bowl combine all ingredients for Topping except walnuts and blend well. Stir in ¾ cup walnuts. Spoon Topping

Golden Pear Drops

1¾ cups Pillsbury's Best All Purpose Flour
  1 teaspoon soda
½ teaspoon salt
¾ cup firmly packed brown sugar
½ cup butter, softened
½ cup dairy sour cream
  1 egg
½ teaspoon peppermint extract
  1 cup chopped canned pears, well *drained*
  1 cup black walnuts or walnuts
¼ cup chopped maraschino cherries, *drained*

OVEN 375°   60 TO 66 COOKIES

In large mixer bowl combine all ingredients except pears, black walnuts and cherries. Blend well with mixer. Stir in remaining ingredients; mix thoroughly.

Drop by teaspoon onto lightly greased cookie sheets. If desired, top with a maraschino cherry half.

Bake at 375° for 15 to 18 minutes. Cool 1 minute before removing from cookie sheet.

Oatmeal Carmelitas

Crust:
  1 cup Pillsbury's Best All Purpose Flour
  1 cup quick-cooking rolled oats
¾ cup firmly packed brown sugar
½ teaspoon soda
¼ teaspoon salt
¾ cup butter, melted

Filling:
  1 cup (6-ounce package) milk chocolate
      or semi-sweet chocolate pieces
½ cup chopped pecans
¾ cup caramel ice cream topping
  3 tablespoons Pillsbury's Best All Purpose
      Flour

OVEN 350°   24 BARS

In large mixer bowl combine all ingredients for Crust. Blend well with mixer to form crumbs. Press half of crumbs into bottom of 11x7-inch pan. Bake at 350° for 10 minutes.

Remove from oven. Sprinkle with chocolate pieces and pecans. Blend caramel topping and flour; spread over chocolate and pecans. Sprinkle with remaining crumb mixture. Bake 15 to 20 minutes longer or until golden brown. Chill 1 to 2 hours. Cut into bars.

over the Filling and sprinkle with ¼ cup walnuts. Bake at 350° for 25 to 30 minutes. Cool; cut into bars.

Glazed Coffee Crescents

   3 cups Pillsbury's Best All Purpose Flour
   I teaspoon baking powder
  ½ teaspoon soda
   I cup sugar
   I cup butter, softened
  ⅓ cup orange juice
   I tablespoon prepared orange peel
   I cup finely chopped walnuts

OVEN 400°   90 TO 96 COOKIES

In large mixer bowl combine all ingredients except walnuts. Blend well with mixer. If desired, chill I hour for easier handling.

Roll out dough, one half at a time, on floured surface to ⅛-inch thickness. Cut with crescent-shaped or round cutter. Place on ungreased cookie sheets.

Bake at 400° for 8 to 10 minutes until delicately browned. Brush Glaze over warm cookies, a few at a time, then sprinkle immediately with walnuts. Let stand until Glaze dries before storing.

Glaze

Combine in saucepan ½ cup sugar, ⅓ cup strong coffee (or 2 teaspoons instant coffee dissolved in ⅓ cup water) and ¼ cup honey. Bring to rolling boil; simmer 5 minutes.

Pink Meringue Clouds

Cookie dough:
   2 egg yolks
  2½ cups Pillsbury's Best All Purpose Flour
   I teaspoon salt
  ½ teaspoon baking powder
  ¾ cup sugar
  ⅔ cup shortening
  ¼ cup milk
   I teaspoon vanilla extract

Peppermint Meringue:
   2 egg whites
  ¼ teaspoon salt
  ½ cup sugar
  ½ teaspoon vanilla extract
  ½ teaspoon vinegar
   I cup (6-ounce package) semi-sweet
     chocolate pieces
   I cup coarsely crushed peppermint stick
     candy

OVEN 325°   42 TO 48 COOKIES

In large mixer bowl combine cookie dough ingredients. Blend well with mixer. Chill while preparing Meringue.

Prepare Peppermint Meringue by beating egg whites in small mixer bowl with salt until soft mounds form. Gradually add sugar; continue beating until stiff peaks form. Fold in vanilla extract, vinegar, chocolate pieces and peppermint stick candy.

Shape dough into balls using a rounded teaspoon for each. Place on ungreased cookie sheets. Flatten with bottom of glass dipped in sugar.

Top each cookie with a rounded teaspoon of Meringue. Bake at 325° for 20 to 25 minutes.

Cherry Bells

Cookie dough:
 2½ cups Pillsbury's Best All Purpose Flour
 ½ teaspoon soda
 ½ teaspoon salt
 I teaspoon ginger
 I cup firmly packed brown sugar
 I cup butter, softened
 I egg
  Maraschino cherries

Coconut-Almond Filling:
 I package (regular size) Pillsbury Coconut-
  Almond Frosting Mix
 ¼ cup butter, softened
 ¼ cup milk

OVEN 375°   48 COOKIES

In large mixer bowl, combine all ingredients for Cookie Dough except cherries until well blended. Place on waxed paper; shape into two rolls 1½ inches in diameter. Wrap; chill several hours or over-night.

Cut into ⅛-inch slices. Place on ungreased cookie sheets.

Combine Filling ingredients in mixing bowl; mix well. Place ½ teaspoon Filling in center of each round. Shape into a "bell" by folding sides of dough together to meet over Filling. Make top of bell narrower than "clapper end." Place piece of maraschino cherry for "clapper."

Bake at 375° for 8 to 10 minutes.

Sweet Pastry Pockets

Crust:
 2 cups Pillsbury's Best All Purpose Flour
 2 tablespoons confectioners' sugar
 ¾ cup butter, softened
 I egg
 2 teaspoons prepared orange peel
 ¼ cup orange juice
  Sugar to sprinkle

Filling:
 ¾ cup almond cake and pastry filling
 ½ cup flaked coconut

OVEN 400°   36 TO 42 COOKIES

In large mixer bowl combine ingredients for crust except granulated sugar. Blend well with mixer to form stiff dough. Chill.

In small bowl combine almond filling and coconut. Blend well. Set aside.

Roll out dough, half at a time, on well-floured surface to ⅛-inch thickness. Cut out with 2½-inch cookie cutter. Place ½ teaspoon Filling in center of each. Fold dough over and seal with a fork.

Place on ungreased cookie sheets. Make a ½-inch cut on top of each for escape of steam. Sprinkle with sugar.

Bake at 400° for 8 to 10 minutes. Cool.

Cherry Dots

2½ cups Pillsbury's Best All Purpose Flour
½ teaspoon salt
I cup sugar
I cup butter, softened
2 tablespoons milk
I teaspoon vanilla extract
34 candied cherries
I cup chopped walnuts

OVEN 350°   96 COOKIES

In large mixer bowl combine all ingredients except cherries and walnuts. Blend well.

Divide dough in two parts. Shape each into a 12-inch roll on waxed paper.

Place 17 candied cherries side by side on top of each roll. Press lightly into dough until centered. Mold dough to cover. Sprinkle ½ cup walnuts evenly over each sheet of waxed paper. Roll dough in walnuts. Wrap and chill at least 4 hours or overnight.

Cut into ¼-inch slices. Place on ungreased cookie sheets.

Bake at 350° for 10 to 12 minutes.

Almond Buttercups

Crust:
2 cups Pillsbury's Best All Purpose Flour
¼ teaspoon salt
½ cup sugar
I cup butter, softened
I egg
I teaspoon vanilla extract

Almond Filling:
I egg
¼ cup sugar
½ teaspoon almond extract
½ cup almond paste

OVEN 350°   36 TO 42 COOKIES

In large mixer bowl combine all ingredients for Crust. Blend well. Line bottoms and sides of tiny muffin cups or tart pans.

Prepare Almond Filling by beating egg in small mixer bowl until foamy. Gradually add sugar and almond extract, beating until thick and ivory colored. Blend in almond paste; mix well. Fill each tart shell with one teaspoon Almond Filling.

Bake at 350° for 20 to 25 minutes until light golden brown. Cool 5 minutes before removing from pans.

Flaky Sweetheart Crescents

Dough:
- *4 cups Pillsbury's Best All Purpose Flour*
- *½ teaspoon salt*
- *I cup butter*
- *3 egg yolks*
- *½ cup dairy sour cream*
- *I package active dry yeast*
- *I teaspoon vanilla extract*
- *Sugar*

Pecan Filling:
- *3 egg whites*
- *I cup sugar*
- *¾ cup finely chopped pecans*
- *I teaspoon vanilla extract*

OVEN 350°   48 COOKIES

In large mixer bowl combine flour, salt and butter. Blend with mixer until particles are coarse. Blend together yolks, sour cream, yeast and vanilla extract. Mix well. Add to flour-butter mixture. Stir to form a dough. Divide into 4 parts.

Roll out each part on surface sprinkled with sugar. Roll to an II-inch circle; cut into I2 wedges.

Prepare Pecan Filling by beating egg whites in small mixer bowl until soft peaks form. Gradually add sugar and continue beating until stiff peaks form. Stir in pecans and vanilla extract. Mix thoroughly. Spread on dough.

Roll each wedge, starting with wide end and rolling to point. Place point-side down on greased cookie sheet, curving ends to form crescent shape.

Bake at 350° for 20 to 25 minutes.

Jamborees

- *3 cups Pillsbury's Best All Purpose Flour*
- *½ teaspoon salt*
- *I cup sugar*
- *I¼ cups butter, softened*
- *I tablespoon milk*
- *2 eggs*
- *2 tablespoons vanilla extract*
- *½ cup apricot preserves*
- *½ cup finely chopped walnuts*

OVEN 375°   60 TO 66 COOKIES

In large mixer bowl combine all ingredients except apricot preserves and walnuts. Blend well with mixer.

Drop by rounded teaspoon onto ungreased cookie sheets. Flatten with bottom of glass dipped in sugar.

Spoon ¼ teaspoon apricot preserves into center of cookie. Sprinkle with walnuts.

Bake at 375° for I0 to I2 minutes until delicately browned.

Fudge Nougats

    1 cup sugar
    ¾ cup Pillsbury's Best All Purpose Flour
    ½ cup butter
    1 (15-ounce) can sweetened condensed
      milk
    1 cup (6-ounce package) semi-sweet
      chocolate pieces
    1 cup graham cracker crumbs
    ¾ cup chopped walnuts
    1 teaspoon vanilla extract
    1 cup miniature marshmallows

40 PIECES

In saucepan, combine sugar, flour, butter and condensed milk. Bring to a boil, stirring constantly; boil 1 minute. Remove from heat. Add remaining ingredients except marshmallows; mix well. Stir in marshmallows. Spread in buttered 12x8-inch pan. Cool. (For faster setting, place candy in refrigerator.)

Peanut Butter Nougats: Substitute 1 cup chopped peanuts for the walnuts; add ¼ cup peanut butter with the chocolate pieces.

Holiday Unbeatables

    2 cups confectioners' sugar
    ½ cup Pillsbury's Best All Purpose Flour
    ½ teaspoon baking powder
    ½ cup (3 to 4) egg whites
    2 cups chopped walnuts
    1 cup chopped candied cherries

OVEN 325°   48 COOKIES

In mixing bowl, combine sugar, flour, baking powder and egg whites. Stir until thoroughly blended. Add walnuts and cherries; mix well. Drop by teaspoon 2 inches apart onto greased and floured cookie sheets. Bake at 325° for 12 to 15 minutes. Let stand 2 to 3 minutes; remove from cookie sheets.

Variations: Substitute 2 cups chopped macadamia nuts, 1 cup flaked coconut and ½ cup chopped candied pineapple for the walnuts and cherries.

Substitute 1½ cups diced toasted almonds and 1½ cups after dinner mints for the walnuts and cherries.

Substitute 2 cups chopped nuts and 1 cup chopped dates for the walnuts and cherries.

Treasure Chest Bars

    2 cups Pillsbury's Best All Purpose Flour
    1½ teaspoons baking powder
    ½ teaspoon salt
    ½ cup firmly packed brown sugar
    ½ cup sugar
    ½ cup shortening
    ¾ cup milk
    2 eggs
    1 teaspoon vanilla extract
    1 cup well-drained maraschino cherry
      halves
    1 cup coarsely broken salted mixed nuts
    4¼-ounce milk chocolate candy bar, cut in
      small pieces

OVEN 325°   36 BARS

In large mixer bowl combine all ingredients except cherries, nuts and chocolate pieces. Mix until well blended. Stir in remaining ingredients, mix well.

Spread in greased and lightly floured 15x10x1-inch jelly roll pan. Bake at 325° for 25 to 30 minutes. Frost while warm. Cool; cut into bars with a sharp knife.

Vanilla Frosting

Prepare 1 package (small size) Pillsbury Buttercream Vanilla Frosting Mix as directed on package.

HIGH ALTITUDE ADJUSTMENT (5200 FEET)
Oven temperature 350°. Decrease baking powder to 1 teaspoon.

Spicy Spritz

  2 cups Pillsbury's Best All Purpose Flour
  1 teaspoon ginger
  1 teaspoon cloves
  1 teaspoon cinnamon
  ½ teaspoon soda
  ½ teaspoon salt
  ¾ cup sugar
  ¾ cup shortening
  1 egg
  ¼ cup molasses
  1 teaspoon lemon extract

OVEN 375°   66 TO 72 COOKIES

In large mixer bowl combine all ingredients. Blend well with mixer.

Press dough through cookie press in long strips, using tooth (spritz) plate, across ungreased cookie sheets.

Bake at 375° for 5 to 7 minutes. Cool 1 minute, cut into 2½-inch strips and remove from cookie sheets.
HIGH ALTITUDE ADJUSTMENT (5200 FEET)
Decrease soda to ¼ teaspoon.

Spicicles

  2½ cups Pillsbury's Best All Purpose Flour
  ½ teaspoon salt
  ¼ teaspoon cinnamon
  ¼ teaspoon cloves
  ¼ teaspoon cardamom
  1 cup confectioners' sugar
  1 cup butter, softened
  1 egg
  1 cup raisins
  ¾ cup chopped walnuts
  ½ cup chopped dates
  ¼ cup finely chopped candied pineapple

OVEN 350°   60 TO 66 COOKIES

In large mixer bowl combine all ingredients except walnuts, raisins, dates, and candied pineapple. Blend well with mixer. Stir in remaining ingredients; mix thoroughly.

Shape into balls using a rounded teaspoon and place on ungreased cookie sheets.

Bake at 350° for 12 to 15 minutes. Cool and roll in additional confectioners' sugar.

Tip: Cookies may be frosted with 1 package (small size) Pillsbury Buttercream Vanilla Frosting Mix and the tops dipped in grated coconut instead of rolling in confectioners' sugar.

Hawaiian Moon Drops

  3 cups Pillsbury's Best All Purpose Flour
  1 teaspoon baking powder
  1 teaspoon soda
  1 teaspoon salt
  ¾ cup firmly packed brown sugar
  ½ cup sugar
  ⅔ cup shortening
  2 eggs
  1 teaspoon vanilla extract
  ¼ teaspoon lemon extract
  ⅔ cup drained crushed pineapple
  1 cup chopped walnuts
  1½ cups toasted coconut

OVEN 375°   48 COOKIES

In large mixer bowl combine all ingredients except pineapple, walnuts and coconut. Blend well with mixer. Stir in pineapple and walnuts; mix thoroughly.

Drop by rounded teaspoon onto greased cookie sheets. Bake at 375° for 12 to 15 minutes. Cool. Frost with Lemon Icing and dip tops in toasted coconut.

Lemon Icing

Prepare 1 package (small size) Pillsbury Buttercream Vanilla Frosting Mix as directed on package, substituting 2 tablespoons lemon juice for water.

Tip: To prepare toasted coconut spread in shallow pan in 350° F. oven stirring frequently until golden brown.

Mincemeat Dream Bars

Cherry Winks

Mocha Butter Balls

Spicy Spritz

Holiday
Unbeatables

Treasure Chest Bars

Spicicles

Fudge Nougats

Hawaiian Moon Drops

Mocha Butter Balls

1¾ cups Pillsbury's Best All Purpose Flour
¼ teaspoon salt
⅔ cup instant chocolate beverage mix
⅓ cup confectioners' sugar
1 teaspoon instant coffee
⅔ cup butter, softened
1 (3-ounce) package cream cheese, softened
2 teaspoons vanilla extract
1 cup chopped pecans
Confectioners' sugar

OVEN 350°   54 TO 60 COOKIES

In large mixer bowl combine all ingredients except pecans. Blend well with mixer. Stir in pecans; mix thoroughly.

Shape dough by rounded teaspoon into balls. Place on ungreased cookie sheets.

Bake at 350° for 15 to 18 minutes. While warm, roll in additional confectioners' sugar.

Cherry Winks

2¼ cups Pillsbury's Best All Purpose Flour
1 cup sugar
2 teaspoons baking powder
½ teaspoon salt
¾ cup shortening
2 tablespoons milk
1 teaspoon vanilla extract
2 eggs
1 cup chopped pecans
1 cup chopped dates
⅓ cup maraschino cherries, drained and chopped
1 cup pre-crushed cornflakes
15 maraschino cherries, cut in fourths

OVEN 375°   60 COOKIES

In large mixer bowl combine flour, sugar, baking powder, salt, shortening, milk, vanilla extract and eggs. Blend well with mixer. Stir in pecans, dates and chopped cherries; mix well.

Drop by rounded teaspoon onto ungreased cookie sheets. Sprinkle with cornflakes; top with a cherry fourth.

Bake at 375° for 10 to 12 minutes.

Mincemeat Dream Bars

1½ cups plus 2 tablespoons Pillsbury's Best All Purpose Flour
¾ cup firmly packed brown sugar
¾ teaspoon salt
½ cup shortening
1½ cups prepared mincemeat
2 eggs
⅔ cup sugar
½ cup instant chocolate malted milk powder
½ teaspoon baking powder
1 cup quick-cooking rolled oats
½ cup flaked coconut

OVEN 350°   36 BARS

In large mixer bowl combine 1½ cups flour, brown sugar, ¼ teaspoon salt and shortening. Blend with mixer until particles are fine. Press in ungreased 13x9-inch pan. Spread mincemeat over crumb crust.

Combine 2 tablespoons flour, ½ teaspoon salt and remaining ingredients in same large mixer bowl. Blend well. Spread over mincemeat. Bake at 350° for 30 to 35 minutes. Cool; cut into bars.

Butterscotch Secrets

Cookie dough:
    ½ cup butterscotch pieces
    ⅓ cup butter
    1½ cups Pillsbury's Best All Purpose Flour
    1 cup confectioners' sugar
    ½ teaspoon soda
    1 egg
    ½ teaspoon vanilla extract

Coconut Filling:
    1 egg white
    ¼ teaspoon cream of tartar
    1 tablespoon sugar
    ¾ cup chopped pecans
    ½ cup flaked coconut

OVEN 375°   46 TO 52 COOKIES

Melt butterscotch pieces and butter in large saucepan over low heat, stirring constantly. Remove from heat. Stir in remaining ingredients. Blend well. Reserve ¼ cup for Filling. Chill remaining dough for easier handling.

Prepare Filling by beating egg white and cream of tartar until soft mounds form. Add sugar and continue beating until soft peaks form. Stir in pecans, flaked coconut and reserved cookie dough.

Shape dough into a 14x4-inch rectangle on waxed paper. Spread Filling down center of dough. Bring dough around Filling, sealing edges. Shape into a roll. Wrap; chill at least 2 hours.

Cut into ¼-inch slices. Place on ungreased cookie sheets. Bake at 375° for 10 to 12 minutes.

Swedish Taffy Creams

    1 cup butter
    1½ cups Pillsbury's Best All Purpose Flour
    1 teaspoon baking powder
    1⅓ cups sugar
    ⅓ cup milk
    ⅓ cup dark corn syrup
    1⅓ cups quick-cooking rolled oats
    1 teaspoon vanilla extract

OVEN 350°   36 TO 42 SANDWICH COOKIES

In large saucepan melt butter over low heat. Remove from heat. Stir in remaining ingredients; blend well.

Drop by scant teaspoon onto greased and floured or teflon cookie sheets. Bake at 350° for 10 to 12 minutes.

Remove carefully from cookie sheet. Just before serving, put two cookies together, sandwich-style, with Frosting.

Butter Cream Frosting

Prepare 1 package (small size) Pillsbury Buttercream Vanilla Frosting Mix as directed on package.

Nut Nibblers

    4 eggs
    1 cup sugar
    1 cup Pillsbury's Best All Purpose Flour
    1 teaspoon vanilla extract
    2½ cups chopped dates
    1 cup chopped pecans
    1 cup stick pretzels, broken into 1-inch pieces
    1 cup doughnut-shaped oat cereal
    1 cup bite size shredded rice biscuits

OVEN 350°   60 SQUARES

In large mixer bowl beat eggs at high speed until light and fluffy. Gradually add sugar; continue beating until thick and lemon colored. Add flour and vanilla extract; blend well. Stir in dates mixing thoroughly. Combine remaining ingredients; set aside 1 cup. Fold remainder into batter. Pour into greased and floured 15x10x1-inch jelly roll pan. Sprinkle with reserved cereal-nut mixture. Bake at 350° for 25 to 30 minutes. While hot, cut into 1½-inch squares. Cool in pan.

Frosted Fruit Jumbles

    4 cups Pillsbury's Best All Purpose Flour
    1 teaspoon salt
    1 teaspoon soda
    ½ teaspoon mace
    ½ teaspoon nutmeg
    ¾ cup firmly packed brown sugar
    ½ cup sugar
    1 cup butter, softened
    2 eggs
    ⅓ cup dairy sour cream
    1 teaspoon lemon extract
    1 teaspoon vanilla extract
    2 cups chopped candied fruit
    ½ cup raisins
    ½ cup chopped walnuts

OVEN 375°   78 TO 84 COOKIES

In large mixer bowl combine all ingredients except fruit, raisins and walnuts. Blend well with mixer. Stir in remaining ingredients; mix thoroughly.

Shape into balls using a rounded teaspoon for each. Place on ungreased cookie sheets. Bake at 375° for 10 to 12 minutes.

Lemon Glaze

Combine 2 tablespoons butter, softened, 2 cups confectioners' sugar and 1 teaspoon lemon extract. Add 2 to 3 tablespoons milk until of spreading consistency.

Danish Tea Drops

    1 cup Pillsbury's Best All Purpose Flour
    ½ teaspoon baking powder
    ½ teaspoon salt
    ⅓ cup sugar
    ½ cup shortening
    1 egg
    2 tablespoons orange juice
    1 tablespoon prepared orange peel
    ¼ cup flaked coconut
    ¼ cup chopped cashews
    ¼ cup semi-sweet chocolate pieces
    Confectioners' sugar

OVEN 350°   30 TO 36 COOKIES

In large mixer bowl combine all ingredients except coconut, cashews, chocolate pieces and sugar. Blend well with mixer. Stir in coconut, cashews and chocolate pieces.

Drop by teaspoon onto lightly greased cookie sheets. Bake at 350° for 10 to 12 minutes. Roll warm cookies in confectioners' sugar.

Missouri Waltz Brownies

    ¾ cup Pillsbury's Best All Purpose Flour
    ½ teaspoon baking powder
    ½ teaspoon salt
    1 cup sugar
    ½ cup shortening
    2 eggs
    2 (1-ounce) envelopes premelted
       unsweetened chocolate
    1 teaspoon vanilla extract
    ½ cup chopped walnuts

OVEN 350°   18 BARS

In large mixer bowl combine all ingredients except walnuts. Blend well with mixer. Stir in walnuts.

Spread in greased 9-inch square pan. Bake at 350° for 25 to 30 minutes. Cool and frost.

Peppermint Frosting

Prepare 1 package (small size) Pillsbury Buttercream Vanilla Frosting Mix as directed on package, adding ⅛ to ¼ teaspoon peppermint extract and 1 drop green food coloring to water.

Candy Bar Cookies

¾ cup butter, softened
¾ cup confectioners' sugar
I teaspoon vanilla extract
2 tablespoons cream
2 cups Pillsbury's Best All Purpose Flour

OVEN 325°   40 COOKIES

Combine all ingredients in large mixer bowl. Mix well with mixer until a dough forms. Pat dough to a 15x10-inch rectangle on ungreased cookie sheet. Bake at 325° for 20 to 25 minutes. Immediately cut into bars. Spread a scant teaspoon of Filling in center of each bar; drizzle with Glaze.

Filling

I cup (6-ounce package) butterscotch
  pieces
2 tablespoons cream
¼ cup confectioners' sugar
I cup chopped pecans

Melt butterscotch pieces in small saucepan over low heat, stirring constantly, until smooth. Remove from heat. Stir in remaining ingredients.

Chocolate Glaze

½ cup semi-sweet chocolate pieces
2 tablespoons cream
¼ cup confectioners' sugar
I teaspoon vanilla extract

Melt chocolate pieces in small saucepan over low heat, stirring constantly, until smooth. Remove from heat. Stir in remaining ingredients.

Tip: For quick and easy layered bars, do not cut into bars after baking. Spread Filling over cookie base; then drizzle with Glaze. Cut into bars.

Chocolate Crunch

½ cup butter
2 cups chopped walnuts
I cup Pillsbury's Best All Purpose Flour
½ cup firmly packed brown sugar
1½ cups confectioners' sugar
½ cup evaporated milk
I to 2 teaspoons peppermint extract
3 (I-ounce) envelopes premelted
  unsweetened chocolate   60 BARS

Melt butter in heavy skillet. Add walnuts, flour and brown sugar; blend well. Continue stirring until crumbs are toasted and golden brown, 5 to 7 minutes. Cool.

In mixing bowl, combine cooled crumbs with remaining ingredients. Blend well. Pour into buttered 9-inch square pan. Chill at least 2 hours. Cut into I-inch bars.

Viennese Tortelettes

2 cups Pillsbury's Best All Purpose Flour
¾ cup sugar
2 tablespoons instant chocolate beverage
  mix
¾ cup butter, softened
2 tablespoons milk
I teaspoon vanilla extract
I teaspoon almond extract
¾ cup (3¾-ounce package) filberts, finely
  chopped
2 tablespoons raspberry jam

OVEN 350°   24 TO 30 SANDWICH COOKIES

In large mixer bowl combine all ingredients except filberts and raspberry jam. Blend well. Stir in filberts, reserving 2 tablespoons for garnish.

Roll out on floured surface, half at a time, to ⅛-inch thickness. Cut into rounds with 2-inch cookie cutter. Place on ungreased cookie sheets.

Bake at 350° for 10 to 12 minutes. Cool. Spread Fudge Frosting between 2 cookies, sandwich-style. Spread top with a thin layer of raspberry jam. Top each with more frosting; sprinkle with reserved filberts.

Fudge Frosting

Prepare I package (small size) Pillsbury Buttercream Fudge Frosting Mix as directed on package.

Quicky Fruitcakes

   I cup chopped walnuts
   I cup raisins
   I cup golden raisins
   I cup chopped dates
   I cup chopped candied fruit
   I cup Pillsbury's Best All Purpose Flour
I½ teaspoons salt
   4 eggs
   I cup firmly packed brown sugar
   I tablespoon prepared orange peel
   I teaspoon vanilla extract

OVEN 325°   48 BARS

In large bowl combine walnuts, raisins, dates and candied fruit. Coat well with ¼ cup flour.

In large mixer bowl combine ¾ cup flour and remaining ingredients. Blend well with mixer. Stir in the fruit and nut mixture, mixing thoroughly. Spread in a greased 15x10x1-inch jelly roll pan.

Bake at 325° for 30 to 35 minutes. If desired, brush while warm with Orange Glaze. Cool; cut into bars.

Orange Glaze

Combine ¼ cup sugar and 2 tablespoons orange juice in small saucepan. Heat, stirring constantly, until sugar dissolves.

Caramel-Nut Acorns

2½ cups Pillsbury's Best All Purpose Flour
 ½ teaspoon baking powder
 ¾ cup firmly packed brown sugar
  I cup butter, softened
  I teaspoon vanilla extract
  I (10-ounce) jar vanilla caramel ice cream
   topping
 ¾ cup finely chopped walnuts

OVEN 350°   54 TO 60 COOKIES

In large mixer bowl combine all ingredients except ice cream topping and walnuts. Blend well with mixer.

Shape into balls using a rounded teaspoon for each. Press each cookie into an acorn shape. Place on ungreased cookie sheets.

Bake at 350° for 10 to 15 minutes. Cool. Dip wide end of cookie in ice cream topping about ½-inch deep and then in walnuts.

Quicky Fruitcakes

Viennese Tortelettes

Candy Bar Cookies

Frosted Fruit Jumbles

Caramel-Nut Acorns

Brazil Nut Melts

I cup Pillsbury's Best All Purpose Flour
½ teaspoon salt
⅓ cup sugar
I teaspoon prepared orange peel
I egg
½ cup shortening
3 tablespoons orange juice or milk
¾ cup chopped Brazil nuts
  Confectioners' sugar

OVEN 350°   36 TO 42 COOKIES

In large mixer bowl combine all ingredients except confectioners' sugar. Blend well.

Drop by rounded teaspoon onto ungreased cookie sheets. Bake at 350° for 10 to 12 minutes. While hot, roll in confectioners' sugar.

Spicy Coffee Shortbreads

2¼ cups Pillsbury's Best All Purpose Flour
1½ teaspoons cinnamon
¼ teaspoon salt
⅓ cup firmly packed brown sugar
⅓ cup sugar
2 tablespoons milk
2 teaspoons instant coffee
I cup butter, softened

OVEN 325°   68 TO 74 COOKIES

In large mixer bowl combine all ingredients. Blend well with mixer.

Press a small amount of dough through a cookie press onto ungreased cookie sheets, using any plate to make desired shapes.

Bake at 325° for 12 to 15 minutes until lightly browned.

Brazil Nut Melts

Spicy Coffee Shortbreads

Nut Nibblers

Swedish Taffy Creams

ocolate Crunch

Butterscotch Secrets

Danish Tea Drops

Missouri Waltz Brownies

121

Norwegian Almond Bars

Date-Orange Toppers

Swedish Heirloom Cookies

122

Date-Orange Toppers

Cookie dough:
  1⅔ cups Pillsbury's Best All Purpose Flour
  2 teaspoons baking powder
  ½ teaspoon salt
  ½ teaspoon nutmeg
  ½ teaspoon cinnamon
  ⅔ cup firmly packed brown sugar
  ½ cup shortening
  2 tablespoons cream or milk
  1 egg
  1 teaspoon vanilla extract
  1 cup quick-cooking rolled oats

Date-Orange Filling:
  ½ cup cut candy orange slices
  ¼ cup water
    dash of salt
  ½ cup chopped dates
  1½ teaspoons cornstarch
  2 tablespoons water

OVEN 375°   42 TO 48 COOKIES

In large mixer bowl combine all ingredients for Cookie Dough. Blend well with mixer. Shape into balls using a rounded teaspoon for each. Place on ungreased cookie sheets.

Prepare Filling by combining in small saucepan all Filling ingredients except cornstarch and water. Cook over low heat until dates are soft, stirring occasionally. Combine cornstarch with water; add to cooked mixture. Continue cooking and stirring until thick and clear. Cool.

Form a hollow in center of each cookie with back of teaspoon. Place a teaspoon of Date-Orange Filling in hollow.

Bake at 375° for 12 to 15 minutes.
HIGH ALTITUDE ADJUSTMENT (5200 FEET)
Decrease baking powder to 1½ teaspoons. Increase cream to 3 tablespoons.

Swedish Heirloom Cookies

  2 cups Pillsbury's Best All Purpose Flour
  ½ teaspoon salt
  1 cup confectioners' sugar
  1 cup butter, softened
  1 (5-ounce) can diced toasted almonds
  1 tablespoon vanilla extract

OVEN 325°   54 TO 60 COOKIES

In large mixer bowl combine all ingredients. Blend well.

Shape into balls or crescents using a rounded teaspoon for each. Place on ungreased cookie sheets.

Bake at 325° for 15 to 18 minutes. Do not brown. Roll warm cookies in additional confectioners' sugar.

Norwegian Almond Bars

Crumb crust:
  2 cups Pillsbury's Best All Purpose Flour
  1 teaspoon baking powder
  1 teaspoon salt
  ¾ cup butter, softened
  ¾ cup sugar

Filling:
  ½ cup Pillsbury Hungry Jack Mashed
    Potato Flakes
  1 (8-ounce) can almond paste
  1¼ cups confectioners' sugar
  ½ cup water
  1 egg
  1 teaspoon cinnamon
  ½ teaspoon cardamom

OVEN 375°   48 BARS

In large mixer bowl combine all ingredients for crust. Blend with mixer until particles are fine. Press half of mixture in ungreased 13x9-inch pan.

Combine remaining ingredients; blend well. Spread over Crumb Crust and sprinkle remaining mixture over Filling. Bake at 375° for 25 to 30 minutes. Cool; cut into bars.

Butternut Balls

2½ cups Pillsbury's Best All Purpose Flour
¼ teaspoon salt
¾ cup confectioners' sugar
1 cup butter, softened
2 teaspoons vanilla extract
1 cup chopped pecans
Confectioners' sugar

OVEN 400°   42 TO 48 COOKIES

In large mixer bowl combine all ingredients except pecans. Blend well with mixer. Stir in pecans; mix thoroughly.

Shape rounded teaspoons of dough into balls the size of walnuts. Place on ungreased cookie sheets.

Bake at 400° for 10 to 12 minutes. Do not brown. While warm roll in additional confectioners' sugar.

Almond Tosca Bars

Crust:
1¼ cups Pillsbury's Best All Purpose Flour
½ teaspoon salt
⅓ cup sugar
⅓ cup butter, softened
1 teaspoon prepared lemon peel
½ cup semi-sweet chocolate pieces

Almond Tosca Topping:
¾ cup chopped almonds
½ cup sugar
⅓ cup light cream
¼ cup butter

OVEN 375°   36 BARS

In large mixer bowl combine all ingredients for crust except chocolate pieces. Blend with mixer until particles are fine. Press in ungreased 8-inch square pan. Bake at 375° for 12 minutes. Do not brown.

Sprinkle immediately with chocolate pieces. Let stand 5 minutes; spread evenly.

Combine in saucepan ingredients for Almond Tosca Topping. Bring to a boil; boil 3 minutes. Pour over chocolate. Bake at 375° for 10 to 12 minutes until lightly browned. While warm cut into bars.

Walnut Frosties

Cookie dough:
2 cups Pillsbury's Best All Purpose Flour
½ teaspoon soda
¼ teaspoon salt
1 cup firmly packed brown sugar
½ cup butter, softened
1 egg
1 teaspoon vanilla extract

Walnut Topping:
1 cup chopped walnuts
½ cup firmly packed brown sugar
¼ cup dairy sour cream

OVEN 350°   42 TO 48 COOKIES

In large mixer bowl combine all ingredients. Blend well with mixer.

Shape into 1-inch balls. Place 2 inches apart on ungreased cookie sheets. Make a depression in center of each cookie.

Combine Topping ingredients and place 1 teaspoonful in each cookie.

Bake at 350° for 12 to 14 minutes or until delicately browned.

Chocolate Layer Cookies

Almond
Tosca Bars

Hawaiian
Fruit Squares

Walnut
Frosties

Butternut Balls

Jam Strip Cheesers

Peanut Blossoms

Chocolate Coated
Cherry-ettes

Icy Walnut Balls

Chocolate Coated Cherry-ettes

2¼ cups Pillsbury's Best All Purpose Flour
½ teaspoon salt
¾ cup confectioners' sugar
 1 cup butter, softened
 1 teaspoon vanilla extract
 1 teaspoon almond extract
½ cup chopped maraschino cherries,
   drained
¼ cup chopped walnuts

OVEN 350°   54 TO 60 COOKIES

In large mixer bowl combine all ingredients except cherries and walnuts. Blend well with mixer. Stir in remaining ingredients; mix thoroughly.

Shape into balls using a rounded teaspoon for each. Place on ungreased cookie sheets.

Bake at 350° for 15 to 18 minutes. Cool. Top each cookie with Frosting.

Chocolate Frosting

Prepare 1 package (small size) Pillsbury Buttercream Fudge Frosting Mix as directed on package increasing water to 3 tablespoons.

Jam Strip Cheesers

2 cups Pillsbury's Best All Purpose Flour
½ teaspoon salt
¼ teaspoon baking powder
¼ cup sugar
¾ cup butter, softened
 1 (3-ounce) package cream cheese,
   softened
 Jam or jelly

OVEN 350°   24 COOKIES

In large mixer bowl combine all ingredients except jam or jelly. Blend well with mixer.

Roll out on floured surface, half at a time, to a 12x3-inch strip. Cut into 3x1-inch strips. Make a deep groove lengthwise down center of each cookie with handle of knife, keeping ends closed.

Place on ungreased cookie sheets. Fill each groove with jam or jelly, using about ¼ cup in all.

Bake at 350° for 20 to 25 minutes.

Hawaiian Fruit Squares

¾ cup Pillsbury's Best All Purpose Flour
 1 teaspoon baking powder
¼ teaspoon salt
¾ cup sugar
 2 eggs
½ cup drained crushed pineapple
½ cup chopped dates
½ cup chopped walnuts
½ cup flaked coconut
   Confectioners' sugar

OVEN 350°   36 SQUARES

In large mixer bowl combine flour, baking powder, salt, sugar and eggs. Blend well with mixer. Fold in remaining ingredients except confectioners' sugar. Spread in greased 9-inch square pan.

Bake at 350° for 25 to 30 minutes. Cool slightly. Cut into 36 squares. Roll in confectioners' sugar.

Chocolate Layer Cookies

    2 cups Pillsbury's Best All Purpose Flour
 ½ teaspoon baking powder
 ½ teaspoon salt
   1 cup sugar
 ¼ cup shortening
 ¼ cup butter, softened
   1 egg
   3 (1-ounce) envelopes premelted
      unsweetened chocolate
 ¼ cup milk
   1 teaspoon vanilla extract

OVEN 400°   42 TO 48 SANDWICH COOKIES

In large mixer bowl combine all ingredients. Blend well with mixer. Chill at least ½ hour.

Roll out on floured surface to ⅛-inch thickness. Cut with 2-inch round cutter; place on ungreased cookie sheets.

Bake at 400° for 6 to 8 minutes. Cool.

Spread half of cookies with Peppermint Frosting. Top with remaining cookies, sandwich-style.

Peppermint Frosting

Prepare 1 package (small size) Pillsbury Buttercream Vanilla Frosting Mix as directed on package, adding 1 drop red food coloring and ⅛ teaspoon peppermint extract.

Peanut Blossoms

    1¾ cups Pillsbury's Best All Purpose Flour
      1 teaspoon soda
 ½ teaspoon salt
 ½ cup sugar
 ½ cup firmly packed brown sugar
 ½ cup shortening
 ½ cup peanut butter
   1 egg
   2 tablespoons milk
   1 teaspoon vanilla extract
 48 milk chocolate candy kisses

OVEN 375°   48 COOKIES

In large mixer bowl combine all ingredients except candy kisses. Blend well with mixer.

Shape into balls, using a rounded teaspoon for each. Roll balls in additional sugar; place on ungreased cookie sheets.

Bake at 375° for 10 to 12 minutes. Remove from oven. Top each cookie immediately with a candy kiss, pressing down firmly so cookie cracks around edge.

Icy Walnut Balls

    1 cup Pillsbury's Best All Purpose Flour
 ¼ cup firmly packed brown sugar
 ⅓ cup butter
   1 cup chopped walnuts
 ¾ cup sweetened condensed milk
   1 teaspoon orange extract
   3 cups confectioners' sugar
   1 cup chopped dates

OVEN 400°   50 COOKIES

In large mixing bowl combine flour, brown sugar and butter. Blend to form coarse crumbs. Stir in ½ cup walnuts. Place in 13x9-inch pan. Bake at 400° for 10 to 12 minutes, stirring occasionally, until crumbs are toasted and golden brown. Cool.

In same mixer bowl combine milk, orange extract and confectioners' sugar. Stir in dates and ½ cup walnuts. Drop by scant teaspoons into crumb mixture. Shape into balls, rolling to coat. Store in refrigerator.

Variation: One cup chopped candied fruit or candied cherries may be substituted for the dates.

Dessert Cookies

• When is a cookie not a cookie? When it is made into a dessert. Brownies cut in larger than usual squares and topped with ice cream and chocolate sauce are favorites with the youngsters.

Spicy bar cookies cut in squares and topped with whipped cream cheese and lemon sauce are an easy-to-fix family dessert.

When you want to impress your bridge club with a fancy dessert, cookies can come to your rescue. Crisp, thin cookies layered with brandy flavored whipped cream, garnished with chopped pistachio nuts and maraschino cherries, and served well chilled will rate a high score. So will chocolate cookie "cups" made by baking cookie rounds on the back of muffin cups. Fill with a scoop of mint ice cream and garnish with chocolate shot or small mint patties.

Party fare or family quickie, here's a selection of easy-to-make cookie desserts to inspire you to create new dessert favorites of your own.

Almond Dessert Towers

1 recipe Almond Party Press Cookies
(pg. 69)
2 cups heavy cream, whipped
2 tablespoons confectioners' sugar
2 tablespoons cocoa
1 tablespoon brandy flavoring
Chopped pistachio nuts
Maraschino cherries

OVEN 350°   16 SERVINGS

Prepare Almond Party Press Cookie dough as directed in recipe, beating until very smooth. Press through cookie press, using flat tooth edge plate, lengthwise across ungreased cookie sheets.

Bake at 350° for 10 to 12 minutes. Immediately cut into 3-inch strips and remove from cookie sheet. Cool.

Fold confectioners' sugar, cocoa and brandy flavoring into whipped cream.

Alternate 5 cookie strips with flavored whipped cream for each dessert tower, topping each with a spoonful of whipped cream. Sprinkle with nuts and garnish with a cherry. Freeze before serving.

Tip: Recipe may be cut in half for 8 servings.

Date Carnival Squares

    I cup chopped dates
⅓ cup water
    2 tablespoons sugar
    2 tablespoons lemon juice
1½ cups Pillsbury's Best All Purpose Flour
½ cup butter, softened
    I cup firmly packed brown sugar
    I egg
    I teaspoon baking powder
    I teaspoon cinnamon
¼ teaspoon soda
¼ teaspoon salt
¼ teaspoon nutmeg
    I cup quick-cooking rolled oats

9 DESSERT SQUARES
OVEN 350°   OR 18 BARS

In small saucepan combine dates, water, sugar and lemon juice. Simmer over low heat, stirring occasionally until thickened. Remove from heat; cool.

In large mixer bowl combine remaining ingredients. Blend with mixer until particles are coarse. Pat half in greased and lightly floured 9-inch square pan. Spread date mixture over base. Sprinkle with remaining crumbs. Bake at 350° for 35 to 40 minutes. Cool; cut into squares.

Golden Teacakes

    2 cups Pillsbury's Best All Purpose Flour
½ teaspoon baking powder
½ teaspoon salt
    I cup butter, softened
1¼ cups sugar
    I teaspoon vanilla extract
    5 eggs
¾ cup raisins
¾ cup golden raisins
    I cup slivered almonds

15 DESSERT SQUARES
OVEN 375°   OR 48 BARS

In large mixer bowl combine flour, baking powder, salt, butter, sugar, and vanilla extract. Blend until smooth. Add eggs, one at a time, beating well after each addition. Fold in the raisins and ½ cup almonds.

Spread in greased and lightly floured 15x10x1-inch jelly roll pan. Sprinkle with ½ cup almonds. Bake at 375° for 20 to 25 minutes. Cool; cut into bars.

Fudge Nut Layer Bars

Filling:
    I cup (6-ounce package) semi-sweet
      chocolate pieces
½ cup sweetened condensed milk
    I tablespoon butter
¼ teaspoon salt
¾ cup chopped walnuts
    I teaspoon vanilla extract

Crust:
½ cup butter
½ teaspoon salt
    I teaspoon vanilla extract
1¼ cups Pillsbury's Best All Purpose Flour
½ teaspoon soda
    I egg
    I cup firmly packed brown sugar
1½ cups quick-cooking rolled oats

OVEN 350°   9 DESSERT SQUARES
OR 36 BARS

In medium saucepan combine chocolate pieces, milk, I tablespoon butter and ¼ teaspoon salt over low heat, stirring constantly until chocolate pieces melt. Stir in ½ cup walnuts and I teaspoon vanilla extract. Set aside.

In large mixer bowl combine ingredients for crust. Blend until particles are coarse. Press half of mixture in greased 9-inch square pan. Spread chocolate filling carefully over base. Sprinkle remaining mixture and ¼ cup walnuts over filling.

Bake at 350° for 25 to 30 minutes. Cool; cut into squares or bars. Top with sweetened whipped cream or ice cream for dessert, if desired.

Butter Cream Bars

1½ cups Pillsbury's Best All Purpose Flour
½ teaspoon salt
¾ cup firmly packed brown sugar
½ cup butter, softened
1 egg
1 cup dairy sour cream
1 tablespoon sugar
1 teaspoon soda
1 teaspoon nutmeg
1 teaspoon cinnamon
¼ cup chopped walnuts

OVEN 350°

9 DESSERT SQUARES
OR 24 BARS

In large mixer bowl combine flour, ¼ teaspoon salt, brown sugar and butter. Blend with mixer until particles are fine crumbs. Press half in a greased 9-inch square pan. Bake at 350° for 10 minutes.

In small mixer bowl combine ¼ teaspoon salt and remaining ingredients except cinnamon and walnuts. Blend well. Spread over partially baked crumb crust. Mix cinnamon and walnuts with reserved crumbs, sprinkle over filling.

Bake at 350° for 35 to 40 minutes. Cool; cut into bars.

HIGH ALTITUDE ADJUSTMENT (5200 FEET)
Oven temperature 375°.

Coffee Toffee Bars

2¼ cups Pillsbury's Best All Purpose Flour
½ teaspoon baking powder
¼ teaspoon salt
1 cup butter, softened
1 cup firmly packed brown sugar
1 to 2 tablespoons instant coffee
1 teaspoon almond extract
1 cup (6-ounce package) semi-sweet chocolate pieces
½ cup slivered almonds

OVEN 350°

15 DESSERT SQUARES
OR 36 BARS

In large mixer bowl combine all ingredients except chocolate pieces and almonds. Blend with mixer until particles are coarse crumbs. Stir in remaining ingredients. Press in greased 15x10x1-inch jelly roll pan.

Bake at 350° for 20 to 25 minutes. While warm, frost. Cool; cut into bars.

Almond Glaze

Combine 1 tablespoon butter, ¾ cup confectioners' sugar and ⅛ teaspoon almond extract. Add 1 to 2 tablespoons milk until of spreading consistency.

Chocolate Refreshers

1¼ cups (8-ounce package) chopped dates
¾ cup firmly packed brown sugar
½ cup butter
½ cup water
1¼ cups Pillsbury's Best All Purpose Flour
¾ teaspoon soda
½ teaspoon salt
½ cup milk
½ cup orange juice
2 eggs
1 cup (6-ounce package) semi-sweet chocolate pieces
1 cup chopped walnuts

OVEN 350°

15 DESSERT SQUARES
OR 36 BARS

In large saucepan, combine dates, brown sugar, butter and water. Cook over low heat, stirring constantly, until dates soften, about 5 minutes. Remove from heat; add remaining ingredients Blend well.

Spread in greased 15x10x1-inch jelly roll pan. Bake at 350° for 25 to 30 minutes. Frost while warm. Cool; cut into bars.

Orange Frosting

Prepare 1 package (small size) Pillsbury Buttercream Vanilla Frosting Mix as directed on package, substituting 2 tablespoons orange juice for water.

HIGH ALTITUDE ADJUSTMENT (5200 FEET)
Oven temperature 375°. Decrease soda to ½ teaspoon.

Lemon-y Layers

I cup plus I tablespoon Pillsbury's Best
  All Purpose Flour
½ cup butter, softened
¾ cup firmly packed brown sugar
⅛ teaspoon salt
2 eggs
¼ cup frozen lemonade concentrate,
  thawed
I teaspoon vanilla extract
1⅓ cups flaked coconut
½ cup chopped walnuts

OVEN 350°

6 DESSERT BARS
OR 24 BARS

In large mixer bowl combine I cup flour, butter and ¼ cup brown sugar. Blend with mixer until particles are fine. Press in ungreased 8-inch square pan.

In same mixer bowl combine remaining ingredients except walnuts. Blend well. Pour over crumb mixture and spread evenly. Sprinkle with walnuts.

Bake at 350° for 30 to 35 minutes. Cool; cut into bars.

Cheesecake Cookies

I cup Pillsbury's Best All Purpose Flour
⅓ cup butter, softened
⅓ cup firmly packed brown sugar
½ cup chopped walnuts
I (8-ounce) package cream cheese,
  softened
¼ cup sugar
I egg
2 tablespoons milk
2 tablespoons lemon juice
½ teaspoon vanilla extract

OVEN 350°

6 DESSERT BARS
OR 16 SQUARES

In large mixer bowl combine flour, butter and brown sugar. Blend with mixer until particles are fine. Stir in walnuts. Reserve I cup for topping. Press remainder in ungreased 8-inch square pan. Bake at 350° for 12 to 15 minutes until lightly browned.

In same mixer bowl combine remaining ingredients. Blend well. Spread over partially baked crust. Sprinkle with reserved crumb mixture.

Bake at 350° for 25 to 30 minutes. Cool; cut into squares.

Peanut Meringue Bars

Crumb Crust:
1½ cups Pillsbury's Best All Purpose Flour
¾ cup firmly packed brown sugar
½ cup shortening
2 egg yolks

Meringue Topping:
2 egg whites
⅛ teaspoon cream of tartar
⅓ cup sugar
⅓ cup firmly packed brown sugar
2 tablespoons Pillsbury's Best All Purpose
  Flour
½ teaspoon vanilla extract
½ cup chopped salted peanuts

OVEN 350°

12 DESSERT SQUARES
OR 24 BARS

In large mixer bowl combine all ingredients for crumb crust. Blend with mixer until particles are fine. Press in ungreased 13x9-inch pan. Bake at 350° for 15 minutes.

To prepare Meringue Topping, beat egg whites with cream of tartar until soft mounds form. Gradually add sugars and continue beating until stiff peaks form. Fold in remaining ingredients.

Spread over partially baked crumb crust. Bake at 350° for 10 to 15 minutes. While warm, cut into bars.

Peanut
Meringue Bars

Lemon-y Layers

Date Carnival
Squares

Golden
Teacakes

Chocolate Refreshers

134

Butter Cream Bars

Fudge Nut Layer Bars

Cheesecake Cookies

Coffee Toffee Bars

135

Chocolate Tartelettes

1 recipe Cocoa Cheese Sandwich Cookies
(pg. 78)
1 quart peppermint stick ice cream
Chocolate shot or chocolate mint candy
wafers

OVEN 350°   12 TO 16 TARTS

Prepare cookie dough as directed in recipe, shaping into a 2-inch roll. Chill.

Cut into slices ⅛-inch thick. Place paper liners on backs of muffin cups. Overlap 3 slices over bottom of paper liners, pressing to seal edges and form cup-shape.

Bake at 350° for 10 to 12 minutes. Cool.

Remove paper liner and fill each "cookie cup" with a scoop of ice cream and garnish with chocolate shot or wafer.

Plantation Dessert Squares

1 recipe Minnesota Harvest Bars (pg. 61)
1 (8-ounce) package cream cheese,
softened
2 tablespoons cream
¼ cup confectioners' sugar
1 package Pillsbury's Lemon Sauce Mix

12 SERVINGS

Prepare Minnesota Harvest Bars as directed in recipe omitting confectioners' sugar.

Blend together cream cheese, cream and confectioners' sugar. Whip until light and fluffy.

Prepare Lemon Sauce Mix as directed on package.

Cut Bars into 12 pieces. Top each piece with a spoonful of whipped cream cheese and warm Lemon Sauce.

Chocolate Tartelettes

Plantation Dessert Squares

Strawberry-Almond Torte

I recipe Almond Buttercups (pg. 110)
I cup heavy cream, whipped
2 tablespoons confectioners' sugar
I tablespoon brandy flavoring
I quart strawberries, washed and hulled

OVEN 350°   8 SERVINGS

Prepare Almond Buttercups crust as directed in recipe. Divide dough in half and press into bottom of two 9-inch round cake pans.

Prepare Almond Filling and spread over crust. Bake at 350° for 25 to 30 minutes until light golden brown. Cool 5 minutes before removing from pans.

Blend confectioners' sugar and brandy flavoring into whipped cream.

Slice half of strawberries and fold into half of flavored whipped cream.

Place bottom layer of torte on serving dish, topping side up. Spread with strawberry-whipped cream mixture. Place second torte layer on top, topping side up. Spoon remaining whipped cream on top. Arrange remaining whole strawberries on whipped cream. Chill before serving.

Index